RUSKIN, BEMBRIDGE AND BRANTWOOD

To my granddaughter

Elizabeth Grace Washington

Ruskin, Bembridge and Brantwood

The Growth of the Whitehouse Collection

James S. Dearden

RYBURN PUBLISHING
KEELE UNIVERSITY PRESS

First published in 1994
by Ryburn Publishing
an imprint of Keele University Press
Keele University, Staffordshire

Text © James S. Dearden

Composition and
monochrome origination by
Ryburn Publishing Services

Printed by
The Amadeus Press
Huddersfield, West Yorkshire
for Ryburn Book Production
Keele University Press
Staffordshire, England

ISBN 1 85331 099 9
Paperback edition

ISBN 1 85331 130 8
Hardback edition

£10

CONTENTS

FOREWORD

The present year sees not only the 175th anniversary of the birth of John Ruskin, but also the 75th anniversary of the founding by John Howard Whitehouse of Bembridge School in the Isle of Wight, and the 60th anniversary of the opening to the public of Brantwood, Ruskin's former home at Coniston in the Lake District. The significance of the second in association with the first will really only be evident to Ruskinians and Old Bembridgians. But it is true to say that Ruskin and Bembridge have both had important effects on each other, albeit indirectly. Today there is little need to remind the reader of the role that Ruskin played in both art and economics in the Victorian era – and indeed in succeeding years. Ruskin's sphere of influence was very wide, and one of the young men who fell under his spell in the 1890s was J. Howard Whitehouse, a clerk working for Cadbury Bros. at Bournville.

Whitehouse discovered the interest and importance of Ruskin; he enthusiastically set about telling everyone else of Ruskin's message and throughout the rest of his life he tried to put Ruskin's teaching into practice. It was in 1919, the year of Ruskin's centenary and the year which saw the exhibition organised by Whitehouse at the Royal Academy to celebrate it, that he founded an independent boarding school for boys at Bembridge in the Isle of Wight. Here he sought to incorporate the best of the old with some of his own and some of Ruskin's educational theories. Literature played a significant part in the school's life; examinations were looked on as relatively unimportant; and there was a great emphasis on creative education. Art, woodwork, printing and music took their places on the timetable and were considered equally as important as maths, science or French.

Whitehouse became well known as an educational pioneer; his book *The School Base*, for example, published in the 1940s, advocated a number of reforms and improvements which were not introduced generally until comprehensive education became fashionable.

Throughout his life Whitehouse continued to champion the Ruskin message; through decades when the name of Ruskin would have been forgotten, Whitehouse and his activities were almost alone in keeping the name alive and in the public eye. Whitehouse was a collector, and from his "discovery" of Ruskin in the 1890s he began buying books, letters, manuscripts, drawings – anything to do with the Master that he could find. At Bembridge he built two beautiful galleries to house part of his collection. He bought Brantwood, Ruskin's home at Coniston in the Lake District, put part of the collection there and opened it to the public.

International academic interest in Ruskin was just beginning at the time of Whitehouse's death in 1955. He had assembled the largest collection of Ruskin material in the world, and in the forty years that have passed since his death almost every international scholar working on Ruskin has visited the galleries at Bembridge. Meanwhile, Brantwood is now a focal point for the visitor to the Lakes, with some 40,000 people going there each year to enjoy its collection, its grounds (which are being restored to their condition in Ruskin's time) and the superb view which prompted Ruskin to buy the house in the first place.

It was decided that, as part of the 75th anniversary celebrations at Bembridge, there should be a major exhibition to show parts of the collection which are not normally seen by the general visitor. The present book began as the catalogue for that exhibition, but it soon took on a life of its own and grew into a history of the collection from the 1890s and a record of Whitehouse's life. Originally, I had planned that it would end in 1955 with Whitehouse's death. However, on reflection it seemed worthwhile to continue the account until the present day, for the collection has continued to grow and develop since 1955, albeit not at the same rate as in the 1930s and '40s.

Perhaps my own first exposure to Ruskin was the quotation on the picture-framer's label on pictures belonging to my parents – "A room without pictures is like a house without windows". Later I was to go to school at Bembridge and thus come under Ruskin's influence. This then brought me into contact with F. J. Sharp and *his* important Ruskin collection. So the present account is partly based on the Whitehouse archive, principally his correspondence with Ralph Brown, and partly on my own records and recollections.

My labour of love has been made easier by the help I have had from various sources. First and foremost I am indebted to The Honourable Mrs E. M. G. Robins, J. P., and her co-directors and trustees of Education Trust Limited and the Whitehouse Trust for their support and permission to reproduce or quote from material at Bembridge and Brantwood. I am also grateful to Mr P. A. H. Brown for agreeing to let me use quotations from his father's letters to Whitehouse, and incidentally to Miss R. M. Collis, who was able to put me in touch with Mr Brown. Dr Robert Hewison kindly agreed to the reprinting from *Ruskin and Venice* of his account of the relationship of the various *Stones of Venice* working papers, while generously reminding me that we had, after all, worked out the relationship together. Mr Evelyn Joll very kindly answered a hypothetical question about the Turners in Ruskin's bedroom. Mr Bruce Hanson and his staff at Brantwood have been very helpful in providing photographs of items in the collection there, and my Isle of Wight photographer, Mr Frank Taylor of Carisbrooke, has, as ever, been most accommodating. I am grateful to Professor Michael Wheeler of the Ruskin Programme at Lancaster University, who helped in many ways while I was unwell. The generous support of The Paul Mellon Centre for Studies in British Art has helped towards the costs of the colour plates in the book. I am particularly indebted to Mr Gerald Taylor, who, at the eleventh hour, very generously helped with the Index. Everyone at Ryburn Publishing and Amadeus Press has worked very hard both to fit a quart into a pint pot *and* meet the publication date. To all of these friends and organisations, I offer my thanks for enabling me to provide this record of one of the achievements of John Howard Whitehouse.

J. Howard Whitehouse, c. 1930

CHAPTER I

THE BEGINNING

John Howard Whitehouse was born at his parents' home, 81 Albion Street, Ladywood, Birmingham, on 8 June 1873. His father George, the son of a blacksmith, was a 25-year-old brass founder at the time of his marriage with Jane Enston on Christmas Day 1869, and their first son, George Oliver, was born in May 1872. At the time of his second son's birth, George Whitehouse was an electro-plate worker.

In his politics George was an uncompromising Gladstonian Liberal, particularly at the time of the Home Rule crisis. For the rest of his life he continued to be dedicatedly opposed to Joseph Chamberlain, whose name he always pronounced "Chamber*lane*". He made a study of the British Empire in India and over the years assembled a library of several hundred books on the subject. Always ambitious to improve his lot, George Whitehouse took the opportunity offered by Forster's Education Act of 1872, which introduced compulsory attendance at school, to take up an appointment as a school inspector.

In his old age, Howard Whitehouse remembered being taken by his father to Birmingham Town Hall to hear what he considered a provocative speech by Chamberlain. He also remembered a visit to the city by Gladstone: the day after addressing a large gathering, he travelled through the streets in an open carriage, and Howard recalled running after the carriage, as long as possible, cheering.

This background was a great influence on Howard to the end of his life. He was a lifelong Liberal, a strong libertarian, an intense believer in the right of the individual to shape his own life, and a bitter opponent of bureaucratic control.

Howard Whitehouse's formal education began at St Mark's Church of England School, which was not far from Monument Road where they lived by this time. Here he first met Edward Organ, and the two were to remain friends for the rest of their lives. St Mark's had an enlightened and progressive headmaster, and the school has a fine record. However, George Whitehouse had differences of opinion with the headmaster, possibly because of the former's hostility to the Tories and later the Unionists, and Howard was removed and sent to a school in Edgbaston.

Whitehouse probably left school at the age of 14, but he continued his education by attending evening classes at the Birmingham Institute and Mason's College. There he acquired the avid interest in literature that he always displayed. A great influence on him at this time was Howard S. Pearson. Pearson had a predominating influence on the cultural life of Birmingham at this period; he was a facile writer, with a graceful and poetic diction – and it seems likely that it was he who first introduced Whitehouse to the writings of John Ruskin.

Whitehouse and Organ attended evening classes together, and writing to me in 1958 Organ said: "J. H. W. must have had an enormous faculty for concentrated study. He astonished everyone by winning the Middlemore prize of five guineas in both literature and history, an achievement that has never been reached before or since. I myself had to be content with a second prize of one guinea in history, and a second prize in French. Perhaps I lacked his concentration. I was studying French, Spanish and German at that time."

Jane and George Whitehouse

Ravenswood, May Vale Road, Bournville

On first leaving school, Howard Whitehouse entered the office of Birmingham chartered accountant Walter Charlton. Organ considered, probably rightly, that this experience was a valuable factor in Whitehouse's development, but he did not remain with Charlton for long, because his father could not afford to pay the necessary fees for his apprenticeship. From the accountant's office, he moved to the firm of saddle-makers, J. H. Brookes & Co. He did not settle there. But it may well have been at this time that he acquired his first books by John Ruskin. Certainly he owned the first edition of W. G. Collingwood's *Life and Work of John Ruskin*, published in 1893, because his early signature occurs at the beginning of each volume.

In 1894, at the age of 21, Whitehouse took a step which was to have a tremendous influence on his future. He joined the firm of Cadbury Bros. as a clerk in the general office. But he found the drudgery of the office irksome, and he was soon showing important visitors around the works. He began a youth club, and the library which he established for it soon became the works library. The youth club's magazine, *Camaraderie*, which he established, developed into the works magazine. He was instrumental in influencing Cadbury's into beginning a "Savings Fund" which grew into the company's pensions scheme.

Monument Road, where Whitehouse lived at this time, was a discreet and respectable area. Edward Organ recalled long rows of neat Victorian houses, with little lawns and iron railings in front, with here and there a fine Georgian mansion. A number of notable people lived in the area, including W. A. Harvey, the architect of much of Bournville village and church. It was to the new village of Bournville that the Whitehouse family moved, from Monument Road, between June and October 1898. They took a house called Ravenswood, in May Vale Road, and later Harvey designed a house – to be called St George's House – for Howard Whitehouse.

Ruskin Society of Birmingham: Syllabus, Annual Report, Minute Book and *St George*

CHAPTER II

THE RUSKIN SOCIETY OF BIRMINGHAM

An announcement in *New Age* on 4 June 1896 advertised a forthcoming meeting "to establish in Birmingham a Ruskin Society on lines similar to the societies already in Glasgow, Liverpool and elsewhere ... a public meeting is to be held shortly, at which Mr E. J. Baillie, the president of the Liverpool Ruskin Society, has promised to be present and deliver an address ... The honorary secretary *pro tem* is Mr J. Howard Whitehouse, of 31 Monument Road, who will be glad to hear from any willing to assist in the movement."

The meeting was duly held at the Midland Institute on 2 July when Edmund J. Baillie spoke; he outlined Ruskin's views on art and science but said that he assumed the new society's chief attention would be focused on Ruskin's political economy. Discussion followed, and the outcome was that the Ruskin Society of Birmingham was established:

1   To form a centre of Union for Students and others interested in Mr Ruskin's writings.
2   To promote the study and circulation of his works by means of Lectures, Discussions, and the issuing of such publications as may be deemed advisable.
3   To influence public opinion, in relation to Arts and Ethics, on lines which he had indicated, and
4   Generally, to encourage such life and learning as may fitly and usefully abide in this country.

A. E. Fletcher, editor of the *New Age*, and formerly editor of the *Daily Chronicle*, was elected first president, and Whitehouse was confirmed as the secretary of the society.

A circular which was issued after the meeting announced that Fletcher's inaugural address would be held in October and subsequent lectures would be delivered on Wednesday evenings throughout the session "at intervals of about a fortnight". It was announced that a library of Ruskin's works was in the course of formation, with Whitehouse's friend Frank T. Rogers as librarian. Edward Organ was appointed treasurer.

The inaugural lecture was eventually delivered on 28 October in the Large Lecture Theatre of Mason's College, Edmund Street, by which time the society had attracted a membership of some 300.

Lectures that season included John C. Kenworthy on "Ruskin's Place in our Social Movement", W. G. Collingwood on *Fors Clavigera*, Howard S. Pearson on *Sesame and Lilies*, Edmund J. Baillie on "The Art of Life, and Mr Ruskin's Views thereon"; two days after Ruskin's birthday the Rev. Edgar Todd spoke on "Ruskin and the Grace of Jesus Christ". Other speakers included Kineton Parkes and Rev. A. Jamson Smith. At the Annual Meeting on 7 April slides lent by W. G. Collingwood were shown and a "descriptive lecture" was delivered by Whitehouse. A. E. Fletcher was succeeded as president by the Very Rev. Charles W. Stubbs, D.D., Dean of Ely, and about six weeks later some 150 members of the society travelled by special train to Ely. They took luncheon at the Bell Inn and were later conducted round the cathedral by the dean.

The society prospered. Lecturers during ensuing seasons included Mrs S. A. Barnett (of Toynbee Hall), Walter Crane, who was to design the society's insignia, Dean Farrar, W. G. Collingwood, Rev.

Ruskin Society excursion to Lincoln, 1899, J. H. W. seated sixth from right

J. Howard Whitehouse,
December 1903

J. P. Faunthorpe (Principal of Whitelands College), Rev. Canon H. D. Rawnsley, Sir Wyke Bayliss, M. E. Sadler, J. A. Hobson, Professor F. York Powell, The Rev. Canon H. Scott Holland, The Very Rev. Francis Paget (Dean of Christ Church, Oxford), F. J. Furnivall, The Very Rev. G. W. Kichin, May Morris, Lionel Cust, Mrs Humphry Ward, Professor W. W. Skeat, Sir Oliver Lodge, Henry Newbolt, and others. In addition to the regular lectures, there were also annual excursions which took the society to Chester (1898), Lincoln (1899), Salisbury (1900) and Oxford (1901).

Not only did Whitehouse occasionally lecture to the society, but throughout this period he was in demand as a lecturer farther afield. For example, in February 1898 he addressed the Ruskin Society of Glasgow on "Some aspects of Ruskin's teaching as applied to Modern Social Problems". In August of the same year he addressed the Whitby Home Reading Union and also spoke at Bangor, while nearer to home in December 1899 he lectured to the Stratford Road Church Literary Society, in Birmingham.

Such was the popularity and success of the Ruskin Society that by the end of the 1903 session the membership stood at 567. Indeed, the council of the Midland Institute lodged a complaint with the University of Birmingham stating that they were suffering serious loss through competition from the society, particularly in the matter of lectures, and there was a move to stop the society using the room made available by the institute after the end of the season. Future meetings were held at the Priory Room, Upper Priory, near the Old Square, Corporation Street.

However, interest in the society declined, and in presenting the twelfth annual report in 1908 the council announced that they had no alternative but to recommend its discontinuance.

In addition to holding its regular lectures and excursions (about 150 lectures between 1896 and 1908), the society became involved in other activities. At the meeting of the council of the society on 27 August 1897 it was resolved that the society should publish a quarterly journal, beginning in the following January. The idea seems to have been Whitehouse's, and it was agreed to leave further arrangements in his hands. At a subsequent meeting it was resolved that the title of the publication should be *St George: The Journal of the Ruskin Society of Birmingham*. The first number appeared in January 1898. In his first editorial note Whitehouse wrote that the journal would not only "preserve the papers and addresses" delivered to the society, but also "chronicle and advance local or national movements which tend to promote the ideas set before us in Mr Ruskin's writings …"

Many of the papers read to the Ruskin Society were printed in *St George*, and in some cases Whitehouse kept the manuscripts, which have survived. For example, on 27 October 1898 Dean Farrar, then the president, addressed the society on "Ruskin as a Religious Teacher". This lecture was originally printed in the second volume of *St George*, in 1899; Whitehouse reprinted it in a revised form in 1904 and a further edition was issued by Arnold Fairbairns in 1907. Farrar's holograph manuscript is now at Bembridge (Bem MS 83), as are the extensively annotated proofs of Professor F. York Powell's "Appreciation of John Ruskin" from *St George*, 1900 (Bem MS 67).

In 1900, F. J. Furnivall, who had known Ruskin from the 1850s, lectured to the society. The lecture, strangely, was not printed, but Whitehouse kept the shorthand notes of the address together with a

J. H. W.'s study at St George's House, Bournville, 1902

transcript of them (Bem MS 73). He also, of course, retained the correspondence files and guard books relating to both the society and *St George*, and they are still at Bembridge.

The scope of *St George* was further broadened in January 1901 when it amalgamated with the new journal of the Ruskin Union (only first published in March 1900). Until this time, *St George* had just paid for itself, but the amalgamation with the *Ruskin Union Journal* resulted in "such a heavy increase in the cost of production as to speedily exhaust the financial resources" of *St George*. The society decided to divest itself of the publication, and responsibility for it was taken on by Whitehouse and "various gentlemen associated with him" (presumably J. A. Dale and Edward McGegan).

As the new publisher of *St George*, Whitehouse adopted the title of The St George's Press. In 1905 it became a limited liability company, with Whitehouse as managing director. The nature of the publication evolved, and after the Ruskin Society was disbanded, it became "A National Review dealing with Literature, Art, Education, and Social Questions in a broad and progressive spirit". It continued until May 1911 when it finally closed with the publication of the 53rd number.

At the committee meeting of the Ruskin Society on 20 January 1899, it was decided to join with the Guild of St George and the

Ruskin Societies of Glasgow and Liverpool in presenting a national address of congratulation to Ruskin on the occasion of his eightieth birthday – 19 days hence. Elsewhere I have shown that the scribe, Albert Pilley of Sheffield, was unable to complete the whole address in the time available, but he *was* able to complete a substantial amount, which was then bound personally by T. J. Cobden Sanderson. Whitehouse and William Wardle, the secretary of the Liverpool Ruskin Society, travelled to Coniston on 7 February to present the address to Ruskin. In his diary for Ruskin's birthday in 1899 Whitehouse wrote:

Feby. 8. The morning was fairly bright and clear and at 11 o'clock we started for Brantwood. It is a glorious road, going for some distance by the margin of the lake and commanding exquisite views. At Brantwood we were very politely received by Mr & Mrs Arthur Severn. They explained that the Master felt equal to seeing us and had expressed a wish to do so. Mr Severn said that he was really wonderfully well and that although we should find him in his bedroom, we were not to conclude from that,

Opening pages of the 1899 Illuminated Address to John Ruskin

Emily Warren's watercolour of Ruskin's bedroom

that he was ill. They did not want him to come down stairs as the staircase was rather narrow, &c. &c. We were then conducted to Mr Ruskin's presence. He was dressed and sitting in an arm chair before a little table. As we entered he attempted to rise, but was evidently too feeble to do so. We shook hands and I told him I was glad to hear he was so well. I then explained that we brought him a national address, and I read it to him. As I was doing so, I occasionally heard him give a low exclamation – half sob it seemed to be. When I had finished he tried to reply but could only utter a few broken words. He was evidently deeply moved and quite overcome with emotion. After he had looked at the address we withdrew and when he had become more composed he dictated to Mrs Severn a reply of which a copy is given at the end of this entry. What most impressed me when I saw the Master were his wonderful eyes. They are blue and very clear and bright. When, during the reading of the address, I looked up at him, I found them fixed upon me as though he were searching me through and through. No one who meets his eyes can doubt that his mind is perfectly clear.

In an article, "At Brantwood, 8th February 1899", in *St George* II, Whitehouse explained that Ruskin was not using his usual bedroom "as owing to the severity of the weather, and the weakness naturally arising from his advanced age, it has been thought wiser for him to remain chiefly in another room, which he temporarily uses both as a sleeping and living room". Whitehouse did not explain which room he meant by "usual bedroom". However, he probably meant the room which is depicted in the paintings by Arthur Severn (Brant 791) and Emily Warren (Brant 803c). Ruskin had probably moved back into the Turret Room, which is a larger room and which he had vacated as his bedroom after his illness in 1878. Whitehouse was later to use this as *his* bedroom at Brantwood.

He did not include the reply dictated to Joan Severn in his diary entry, but he did print it in his *St George* article. She had written: "Mr Ruskin is deeply touched by the Address, and finds it difficult to give expression to his feelings of gratitude, but trusts that they will be made known for him. He values the address highly, and thinks it charmingly done."

Before Whitehouse and Wardle left Brantwood, they had to recover the address from Ruskin in order that Pilley could complete his work, and it was finally taken back to Brantwood by the secretary of the Glasgow Ruskin Society, William Sinclair, whose original idea it had been, in August 1899.

"The Master is dead. Know ye not that there is a Prince and a Great Man fallen this day in Israel." Thus Whitehouse recorded Ruskin's death in his diary on 20 January 1900, and three days later he was off to Coniston again, this time to represent the society at the Master's funeral.

I left tonight for Coniston to attend the Funeral. I travelled all night reaching Coniston soon after 9 on Wednesday morning [24 January]. Put up at the Waterhead Hotel. The coffin was brought from Brantwood at 11 o'clock & I joined the procession as it passed the hotel, travelling in one of the carriages to the Church, bearing with me the Society's wreath which I placed upon the coffin in the Church. Here the coffin will lay in state until tomorrow morning. In the evening Geo: Allen, the Master's publisher, arrived, with his son. Allen evidently feels the loss most keenly & has greatly aged within the last few days. In the evening I had a long & most interesting conversation with him. He commenced telling me many of his reminiscences of Ruskin & in talking seemed to lose himself in his subject. I was indeed surprised that he should have told me many of the things which he did.

He dealt with the divorce between Ruskin and his wife who afterwards became Lady Millais. He stated that the allegations made by the latter were untrue entirely. (The allegations referred to Ruskin's physical inability to consummate the marriage.) Had Ruskin liked he could have prevented the divorce being obtained, but he said to Allen "Had I done so I should have had the woman on my hands for life." The truth was, said Allen, that from shortly after the marriage Mrs Ruskin appears to have been maturing plans for getting away from her husband. Millais was a frequent visitor to Ruskin & took advantage of these visits to get more and more intimate with Mrs Ruskin until the climax came. When the case came before the Ecclesiastical Court Ruskin would have nothing to do with it & went abroad.

At the meeting of the council of the society on 22 February 1900 "the question of a national memorial to the late Master was considered". Writing to me on 24 February 1958, Edward Organ said "The founding of Ruskin Hall was due to the Quixotic genius of J.H.W." Whitehouse's Ruskin memorial scheme was for the erection of a "village library, art gallery, and museum, which will place at the disposal of those living in the country some of those educational and higher influences, which for the most part have now to be sought for in the larger towns".

The village chosen was Bournville, to which Whitehouse had moved in 1898 and where George Cadbury had begun his housing experiment in 1895. George Cadbury gave the site for the memorial and generously donated £500 to the appeal; his nephew Barrow Cadbury gave £100 and Whitehouse himself gave £25, which must have been a huge amount at that time for a clerk of 27 years of age. In an undated circular letter of October 1902 Whitehouse reported that £1,500 had been promised, a further £3,500 was needed, and the foundation stone was to be laid by Lord Avebury on 21 October 1902. A little over a year later the society's committee met to "receive a proposal to transfer the Memorial Building and site to the trustees of the Bournville Village Trust". The society had been unable to raise enough money and it had insufficient funds itself to finance the venture. But the memorial scheme had been a success. It had provided a village centre for the development and furtherance of Ruskin's principles. The architect of the building was W. A. Harvey, with whom Whitehouse would be associated later, at Bembridge. The building was enlarged in 1903 and in 1911 Ruskin

Ruskin Hall, Bournville

Presentation bookplate in
J. H. W.'s set of the Ruskin
Library Edition

Hall became the home of the Bournville School of Arts and Crafts – an organisation which continues to flourish.

In fact, the notice convening the meeting of the committee at which it was decided to hand over the memorial scheme to the Bournville Village Trust is the last item in the society's guard book kept by Whitehouse. On 12 November 1903 he was appointed the first secretary of the Carnegie Dunfermline Trust, an appointment which he took up at the beginning of the following year. On 25 November he resigned the secretaryship of the Ruskin Society and on 18 December the society held a reception at the Royal Society of Artists to say "Goodbye" to him. Presentations were made. An illuminated address, thanking him for his work on behalf of the society and wishing him well in Dunfermline, was commissioned. It was written and illuminated by Miss Evelyn Holden and bound in full vellum gilt by the Birmingham Guild of Handicraft. Signatories included Mrs Craigie, the president of the society, the Bishop of Oxford, George Cadbury, Clarkson Booth, Edward Organ, and his father George Whitehouse. Publication of the new Ruskin *Library Edition* had already been announced; the first volume had been published on 27 March 1903. The society subscribed to a set for their retiring secretary, and Miss E. G. Butler designed a bookplate. Although Whitehouse was to own several further sets of the *Library Edition*, this presentation set was the one which remained in his study and which he used throughout his life – and which is used today by the present writer!

CHAPTER III

FROM BIRMINGHAM TO BEMBRIDGE,

1903–1919

In August 1903 Andrew Carnegie established the Carnegie Dunfermline Trust (he had been born in Dunfermline) with the gift of Pittencrieff Park and Glen, and $2,500,000 in 5% Bonds, giving an annual revenue of £25,000.

It was as secretary of the trust that administered this gift that Whitehouse left Birmingham and took up his duties in Scotland on 1 January 1904. On more than one occasion he stayed at Skibo Castle, Carnegie's home in Dunfermline. I remember Whitehouse's stories of being roused from sleep in the morning by the organ in the hall below being played louder and louder, and of the piper on the terrace during dinner.

At the trust he found a friend and like-thinker in Patrick Geddes, but he was soon at loggerheads with the other trustees over how the funds should best be spent for the benefit of the people of Dunfermline, and on 2 September he resigned his secretaryship. He seems to have returned to St George's House, Bournville, and concentrated his efforts on the St George's Press, the establishment of which was referred to earlier.

The period 1904–5 saw the publication by the St George's Press of a number of pamphlets – Farrar's *Ruskin as a Religious Teacher* (1904), J. L. Paton's *English Public Schools* (1905), F. York Powell's *John Ruskin and Thoughts on Democracy* (1905), Patrick Geddes's *The World Within and the World Without* (1905), and Whitehouse's first book, *Problems of a Scottish Provincial Town* (1905).

Toynbee Hall, the Universities' settlement in East London, was the brainchild of Canon Samuel Barnett. It opened on Christmas Eve 1884 and for over a hundred years it has maintained its role as a residential community living and working in one of London's deprived areas and promoting such ventures as the Workers' Educational Association and the Whitechapel Art Gallery.

Canon Barnett was warden of Toynbee Hall from its foundation until 1906. Between 1903 and 1905 he was helped by William

Staff of Toynbee Hall, 1905–6. Seated from the left are: J. H. W. (2), Canon S. A. Barnett (4), and T. E. Harvey (5)

Beveridge (later the author of the Beveridge Report and architect of our Welfare State) as sub-warden and, from July 1904, by T. Edmund Harvey as deputy warden. Whitehouse joined this team at the beginning of the autumn term, in October 1905, as secretary of Toynbee Hall. His appointment was welcomed with enthusiasm by the *Toynbee Record*, a publication he was to edit from the following year until 1908. 1906 saw the retirement of Barnett, with T. E. Harvey replacing him as warden. In Harvey, Whitehouse found another lifelong friend. They were both Companions of Ruskin's Guild of St George, Whitehouse being elected in 1902 and Harvey very soon afterwards. Whitehouse was to become a trustee of the guild in 1918, with Harvey as the master from 1934 to 1950. This same year saw the development of Whitehouse's interest in young people. He established The National League of Workers with Boys, which was to arrange annual summer camps for deprived secondary-school boys for many summers to come, beginning with a camp in the grounds of Ruskin School at Heacham in Norfolk in 1907. 1906 also saw Whitehouse becoming a manager of East London Schools and being elected to the committee of the Ruskin Union, the secretaryship of which he would assume in 1909.

J. H. W. at one of his summer camps

Whitehouse seems to have lived a full and happy life at Toynbee Hall, and when he left there in August 1908 it seems to have been as the result of a misunderstanding. From East London he went to Harpenden as sub-warden of St George's School, an appointment which would bring him into closer contact with the education of boys. When he went to Harpenden he clearly believed that he would soon be appointed warden. However, there was some confusion, as he had not realised that his appointment was only a temporary one during the absence of the warden. Thus, in the following year he applied for and obtained the post of warden of the University Settlement at Ancoats, Manchester. Ancoats he described as "a district fouled by pestilential factories – pestilential because they emit filth and smoke without hindrance, rendering impure the district around them. It is a district fouled too by squalid unhealthy houses, gardenless and desolate." Those close to him believed that under his leadership the settlement was on the verge of great developments, and indeed he wrote: "I hoped that the Settlement of which I was in charge did something to help the people around – perhaps through its educational, social and medical activities it brought a little health and joy and hope into their lives."

While at Ancoats Whitehouse also very nearly became involved with the beginnings of the Boy Scout Movement. Baden Powell suggested that his scheme should be placed in the hands of White-house's National League of Workers with Boys and arrangements were completed for Whitehouse to become the editor of *The Scout*. The plan was abandoned, however, owing to financial and other difficulties. Baden Powell went on to write his *Scouting for Boys*, while in 1911 Whitehouse published his *Camping for Boys*.

But politics called. The Liberal government of Asquith, irked by the rejection of their 1909 budget and by the treatment of their Parliament Bill, decided to go to the country in January 1910 and Whitehouse was elected as the Liberal member for the mining constituency of Mid-Lanark, which he continued to represent until November 1918. Elected to represent West Leeds in the same parliament was T. E. Harvey. In the House of Commons Whitehouse's energy, command of the written word and his sense of atmosphere made him an ideal parliamentary private secretary, and in this capacity he served C. F. G. Masterman, who was Churchill's Under-Secretary at the Home Office (1910–13), and Lloyd George at the Exchequer (1913–15). He was a member of numerous committees and commissions, especially those dealing with child labour and reformatory work.

During the Balkans War in 1912 he visited that country on a fact-finding mission, probably representing Noel Buxton M.P. The copy in Whitehouse's library of Buxton's subsequent book, *With the Bulgarian Staff*, is inscribed "To the real author (J. H. Whitehouse) from the supposed one."

A couple of years later, in the first few weeks of the war, in 1914, he visited Belgium in order to ascertain the conditions of the civil population in the fighting and devastated areas. He was received by the King of the Belgians, and his subsequent book, *Belgium in War*, contained an introduction by Lloyd George. As a result of his experience with Balkan refugees, he was appointed a commissioner for Belgian refugees in this country.

Also in 1914, in keeping with his interest in youth, he became the editor of that popular paper for boys, *The Champion*. One of the issues contained a series of photographs taken in the Balkans and reproduced in Buxton's book, and eight issues contain the serial by the editor, "Percy Geddes, a Public School Tale".

Whitehouse's secretaryship of the House of Commons Commit-tee for Women's Suffrage may well not have enhanced his political career. But he did greater harm to his parliamentary life in 1915. The growing pressure of the war and its impingement on the liberty of the individual offended his Gladstonian principles and the proposal to introduce conscription found him a bitter opponent. He finally severed his connection with Lloyd George when in November 1915, in company with C. E. H. Hobhouse and Percy Alden, he put his name to a *Statement of a Committee of Members of the House of Commons on the Subject of Conscription*. Though not a conscientious objector himself, he did much good work in Parliament on their behalf, and also on behalf of families suffering severe hardship as a result of conscription.

In 1916 and again in 1917 he went to the United States at the invitation of Colonel House, President Wilson's adviser, to discuss the possibility of a negotiated peace; though the mission failed, this and later visits convinced Whitehouse of the urgent necessity for the Old World to endeavour to know and understand the New World.

The Khaki Election of 1918 found him without a constituency. In the minor revision of constituencies that took place, Mid-Lanark disappeared and Whitehouse unsuccessfully contested neighbouring Hamilton. This defeat had wide-reaching effects. It made him decide to undertake something that had long been in his mind, the foundation of a boarding school on different principles from those underlying the more orthodox public schools.

Just before the outbreak of the war, Whitehouse had met Edward Daws, who introduced him to the Isle of Wight. As a result, in 1914 he bought a field overlooking Whitecliff Bay near Bembridge as a permanent site for his secondary-school boys camp. In the following year the large adjacent house, which he called Yellowsands, came onto the market and he bought it.

It was thus that Bembridge School was established in 1919 to put into effect some of Whitehouse's theories of education and some of Ruskin's, the underlying principles being success through skill and hard work, the dignity of labour and the equal importance of craftsmanship and academic studies. The school opened – with five boys – on 16 May 1919. Whitehouse was the headmaster, or Warden, which was the title he adopted and by which, after this date, he was almost universally known.

During the period between leaving Bournville and moving to Bembridge, Warden's collection continued to grow steadily. He was a Ruskinian and a collector at heart – and he used his collection in connection with the work of the school. But it was his *own* collection and he did not keep formal records. Thus we are uncertain when some of the items were acquired and where they came from. He would no doubt have kept abreast of current publications, for example Spielmann's *John Ruskin* (1900), Collingwood's *Ruskin Relics* (1903), George Allen's *Copyright and Copy-Wrong* (1907), E. T. Cook's *Homes and Haunts of John Ruskin* (1912) and his *Life of John Ruskin* (1911), and Peggy Webling's *A Sketch of John Ruskin* (1914). In fact, during this period more was being published in Japan than in Britain – but Whitehouse would almost certainly have been unaware of this.

One of the books which he did own by now was A. C. Swinburne's copy of *Ethics of the Dust* (1866), inscribed by the author to the poet. It may well have been bought as a result of the sale at The Pines in 1914. Certainly we know that by 1917 he owned a group of ten letters from Ruskin to Rose La Touche's mother Maria (Bem B X), because he published them as "Ruskin in old age. Some unpublished letters" in *Scribner's Magazine* in December of that year.

The first actual record of purchases at Bembridge are marked in a catalogue of a Red Cross sale held at Christie's in 1918. There he bought the corrected proof sheets (lot 2863) of "The Pleasures of Deed" (Bem MS 63), chapter III of *The Pleasures of England*, a lecture delivered at Oxford on 1 and 3 November 1884. The proofs contain a number of holograph corrections and were given to the sale by J. W. Mackail. Interestingly, the fly-leaf is annotated by Ruskin

Ruskin's inscription to Swinburne in *Ethics of the Dust*

"For Reporter. Note corrections at end if you use it." Whitehouse had the sheets bound in green morocco by C. & C. McLeish, a London binder he used at this time. He also had a similarly bound set of unmarked proofs of "The Pleasures of Learning" (Bem MS 64), the first lecture in *The Pleasures of England* series. This does not appear to have come from the same sale, but we may assume that he acquired it at about the same time.

Also in this Red Cross sale he paid £14 for lot 2164, seven letters written by Ruskin to his Scottish friend William Macdonald (Bem L 25), subsequently publishing six of them in 1920 in *Ruskin the Prophet* in a chapter titled "Ruskin and an early friendship". The following lot 2165 also fell to Whitehouse. He paid £21 for a series of eleven letters to Jemima Blackburn (Bem L 25). This correspondent was a talented amateur artist and some of the letters contain helpful advice from Ruskin.

Isabella Jay was a professional copyist specialising *almost* exclusively in Turner. Ruskin noticed her copying a Turner in the National Gallery in the 1860s and he praised her work. In a lithographed circular dated 4 January 1868 Ruskin wrote: "Miss Isabella Jay's copies of Turner's pictures are the most accurate and beautiful I have yet seen, in many respects attaining fully to the expression of the master's most subtle qualities; and I think that such copies are much more valuable and instructive possessions than the original drawings of second-rate artists."

Miss Jay always remained independent. She was never formally an artist working for the Guild of St George, although her copy made in 1885 of T. M. Rooke's "Hillside view near Cluse" is in the collection at Sheffield. Ruskin also had a number of her copies of Turners in his collection at Brantwood. Several of them would ultimately come to Bembridge through the Sharp collection.

Whitehouse originally met Miss Jay at Whitelands College in Chelsea in 1912, where Ruskin had established a May Queen's Ceremony in 1881. It is not clear whether or not they had both been guests at the installation of Queen Alice in 1912, or whether they had met at a meeting of the Ruskin Union which, thanks to the principal, the Rev. J. P. Faunthorpe, held occasional meetings at Whitelands.

It is possible that Whitehouse may have bought examples of Miss Jay's work from her. In all, Bembridge now has 26 of her copies. What is certain is that when she died on 21 July 1919 she

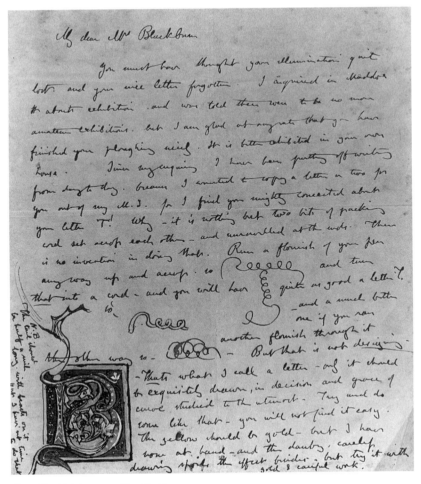

One of Ruskin's letters to Mrs Blackburn

bequeathed 19 of her copies to him. The list included her copies of one of the 1882 Elliot and Fry photographs of Ruskin (Brant 738), of Memling's Duke of Cleaves (Bem 263) and Titian's Truth (or Sacred and Profane Love – Bem 264).

Copies of Turners included the large Funeral of Sir David Wilkie (Brant 737) and Hastings (Bem 268). The bequest also included "6 watercolours (pure) and 6 grey paper watercolours"; these are probably Bem 281 and 282 and Brant 736, 739, 740 and 741 – three of them studies of Venice, and Bem 265, 269, 270, 272, 279, 280, the smaller blue paper copies. Also included in the bequest were two drawings described as "No. 22 and No. 23". These cannot be positively identified, but may well have been copies of Turner's

St Gothard (Bem 276) and Petworth Park, Tillington Church in the Distance (Bem 271), both of which are known to have been in the collection for some considerable time.

In addition to founding a school in 1919, Whitehouse was also busily engaged as the principal organiser of the Ruskin Centenary Exhibition, held at the Royal Academy between 1 October and 22 November. This could not have been an easy task, because *some* of the material in the exhibition was in the Centenary Exhibition at Coniston between 21 July and 20 September. As well as the exhibition, Whitehouse arranged a series of lectures by Arthur Severn, W. G. Collingwood, John Masefield, Bernard Shaw and others. I have written elsewhere of the publication by Whitehouse of these various lectures.

The catalogue of the Academy exhibition is valuable in indicating the scope of Whitehouse's collection in 1919. In addition to the 1918 purchases enumerated above, Whitehouse also exhibited material relating to the Birmingham Ruskin Society – files, minute books, manuscripts of lectures by Mackail (Bem MS 67), Inge (Bem MS 79), H. W. Nevinson (Bem MS 67), and various printed books, including the Kelmscott *Nature of Gothic* and the Doves *Unto this Last*.

Also exhibited by Whitehouse in the Centenary Exhibition was a collection of a hundred letters written by Ruskin to his assistant and eventual publisher, George Allen (Bem B II–IV). These letters span the period 1857 to 1872 and seem to be a random selection from the many hundreds originally in the series. These are bound in full calf gilt by Sangorski and Sutcliffe in three volumes. Each volume has a handwritten title page, and bound in at the front of the first volume is a nine-page note about George Allen written by his son William S. Allen and dated from the Allens' home at Sunnyside, Orpington, Kent, in September 1915. Each original letter is tipped into a recessed leaf of card and is followed by a typed transcript of the original, some edited with footnotes by William Allen.

William Allen was obviously intent on selling the Ruskin material which the family had inherited to the best advantage! I have seen seven further volumes of the Ruskin–Allen correspondence, similarly bound, in the Butler Library at Columbia University, New York, and I have seen a much smaller collection of material relating to Allen and the Guild of St George, again with a similar title page and binding, in a private collection in Japan. In January 1921 Charles J.

John Ruskin's self-portrait,
1874

Sawyer offered Whitehouse a further 64 letters in the same series, written between 1859 and 1888, but he did not buy them.

By the time of the 1919 exhibition Whitehouse had well and truly laid the foundations of his collection of watercolours and drawings, including 22 which he had bought at the sale of part of Charles Eliot Norton's collection. These included a view of the Alps from Munich (Brant 959), a study from Carpaccio's St George (probably Bem 1195), Head of Solomon after Veronese (Bem 1671), and a sketch inscribed by Ruskin to Norton "You know where this is! Keep it for yourself. J. R. 1879", which Anthony Harris has recently identified as one of the lion waterspouts on the façade of the Fontebranda in Siena (Bem 1359). But the most important drawing in the collection at this time was one of the pair of self-portraits – the pencil drawing – which Ruskin made for Norton in 1874 (Brant 991).

It is clear that by the time Whitehouse founded Bembridge School and came to live in the Isle of Wight he had already begun to build a substantial collection of Ruskin material.

CHAPTER IV

CONTINUED GROWTH, 1920–1930

To say that the years 1920 to 1930 were busy ones for Whitehouse would be misleading, for *all* years were busy ones for Whitehouse!

The school which he had founded at Bembridge grew in both numbers and physical size, new buildings being added whenever numbers demanded or finances permitted. One of the first of the new buildings was a school museum. Known as the Ruskin Museum, it was situated immediately inside the school gates, symbolically uniting the school and the village. The original design was by Baillie Scott, but the plans were considerably modified by Stephen Salter and the museum was completed by the Christmas term of 1920. Although called the Ruskin Museum, it did not in fact house Whitehouse's Ruskin collection, but provided the space for a regular series of temporary educational exhibitions. Many of Whitehouse's ideas about education were new and they received considerable support. The National League of Workers with Boys was merged with the newly formed Society for Experiment and Research in Education and, through this vehicle and its annual lecture, Whitehouse was able to obtain publicity for Bembridge. Meanwhile, many of his former parliamentary friends were summoned to help open buildings, make speeches, serve on committees, or even send their children to the school – friends like Isaac Foot, C. F. G. Masterman, Percy Alden, and others.

Whitehouse's interest in America continued, and indeed the study of American history was a compulsory part of the timetable. In 1921 he had a series of talks in London with Colonel House, with whom he had been negotiating during the war. In that year he had addressed the Society for Research in Education on "American Experiments in Education", and five years later he presented an exhibition illustrating English education to New York University – which elected him a fellow; meanwhile in 1922 he was appointed a governor of the Sulgrave Institution.

School journeys were arranged, and Whitehouse accompanied

parties to Venice, to Rome, Holland, Oberammergau and Fribourg. A visit to Oslo in 1928 to present explorer and statesman Fridtjof Nansen with a relief model of his journey "Farthest North" led to the revelation that Nansen's ship, *Fram*, was gradually rotting in an Oslo fjord. On his return to England Whitehouse established the Committee for the Preservation of the *Fram*, which raised some funds in this country but, more importantly, was instrumental in persuading the Norwegians themselves to do something about the ship. As an outcome the *Fram* was preserved, and the museum built to house her developed into a national maritime museum housing several Viking ships, the Kontiki raft and other vessels. Whitehouse's part in this was recognised in 1932 when he received the Norwegian order of a Knight of the Order of St Olav.

Meanwhile politics still attracted Whitehouse; how he would have run the school had he returned to Parliament is in doubt, but at general elections he contested Hanley (1922), Hereford (1923 and 1924), Southampton (1929), Thornbury, Gloucestershire (1931), and Stoke Newington (1935). He was always defeated, but he used his campaigns to introduce a number of Bembridge boys, such as Dingle Foot, a future solicitor-general, to the hustings.

There were personal troubles. His brother Oliver died in 1922, leaving a widow and a daughter. Three year later his father died at the age of 79. Eventually Whitehouse's mother moved from Bournville to live near her son at Bembridge. She was to die in 1927.

Seldom did a year pass without at least one book – and often several – written or edited by Whitehouse appearing on the market. Ruskin, education and Nansen were the subjects. In fact, so many books went out under his name that by the end of his life he had the second longest entry in *Who's Who*, largely because of his lengthy list of publications. And amid all this activity the quest for Ruskin was pursued relentlessly. By early 1920 (although almost certainly after the Centenary Exhibition) a group of half a dozen letters from Ruskin to George Jones, secretary to the Royal Academy, and one from J. M. W. Turner to Jones was bought (Bem B XI). The Ruskin letters were published as "Some early friends and contemporaries of Ruskin" in *The Athenaeum* of 26 March 1920.

Meanwhile William Allen had offered Whitehouse a group of Ruskin manuscripts in December 1919 – *Lectures on Architecture and Painting* (£260), *The Two Paths* (£260) and fragmentary manuscripts or proofs for ten other books – all of which must have been declined. It is not clear whether the Ruskin–George Allen correspondence included in the Centenary Exhibition had come directly from William Allen as an earlier transaction. But demand for Ruskin really had fallen! On 25–26 July 1921 the Severns, who were always chronically short of money, offered 16 lots of Ruskin manuscripts for sale at Sotheby's. The most substantial was a group of 206 pages of the *Fors Clavigera* manuscript. Bidding for this reached £31. The total bid for the 16 lots was £37 5s., and it seems probable that most of the lots were bought in. Certainly the manuscripts from this sale which are now in the Bembridge collection formed part of lot 119 in the later Brantwood sale in 1930 at which Whitehouse bought them. There are revised proofs and 23 pages of manuscript for *The Eagle's Nest* (Bem MS 56/A), *The Three Colours of Pre-Raphaelitism*, 10 pages (Bem MS 51/K), *Elements of English Prosody*, 5 pages (Bem MS 62), *Trapping of Strudi*, 4 pages (Bem MS 51/N) and *Letter on Railways in Derbyshire*, 5 pages (Bem MS 51/P).

The February 1923 issue of *The Beacon* included an article by Whitehouse on "Ruskin's First Sketch-Book", which presumably he had acquired recently or at least since 1919. Ruskin described this "inconvenient upright small octavo in mottled and flexible covers" in *Præterita*. It contains, among other sketches, "My first tree from nature". In later life Ruskin dismembered the volume, giving two sketches of Canterbury Cathedral – the south porch and the central tower – to Miss Gale of Canterbury. The remainder of the volume, which Whitehouse had bought, had been given to Mrs Fanny Talbot, an early benefactor of both the Guild of St George and the National Trust. Whitehouse must have been pleased to be able eventually to buy the two detached drawings for his collection and reunite them with the rest of the book.

Joan Severn, who with her husband Arthur had inherited Brant-wood and its contents from Ruskin, died at Brantwood in 1924. After Joan's death, Arthur spent more and more time at his London house in Warwick Square; however, he was at Brantwood in the following year when Whitehouse stayed there with him for a few days. There was a plan for the Guild of St George to take over the house and estate "as a place of pilgrimage for ever in honour of the Master". Whitehouse spoke of this visit in one of his Bembridge School Chapel addresses:

It was my privilege to live for a couple of days in the room which had been Ruskin's. I was able to go from this room into a little turret which he had built. It had five sides. He had built it leading from his room in order that he might walk from his bedroom and see south, north and east, up and down and across the lake, and the glory of the sunrise. I was able also to see some of the treasures which he had amassed for the use and enjoyment of others; pictures by the great masters, minerals, books, illuminated manuscripts, rare coins. I saw too great numbers of his own drawings and sketches, all of them showing his wonderful patience in sketching for the delight of other things in nature and art which had for him a deeper meaning than for many, but which through him others have been led to appreciate.

Whitehouse had first met Severn in 1899, of course, when he had taken the Birthday Address to Ruskin, and he was in touch with him again in connection with the Centenary Exhibition. This attempt to negotiate with Severn over the purchase of Brantwood – which continued sporadically for the next two or three years – was just one of several dealings the two had together. "If you come here again", wrote Severn to Whitehouse from Warwick Square on 26 August 1927, "I could have those Ruskin drawings ready for you to take back" (BEM L 68). A month later Whitehouse offered Severn £90 for "the little book" which he had seen, and in his reply on the following day Severn confirms that this was a "missal". Ruskin had a fine collection of medieval manuscripts, many of prime quality. The sale of these provided the Severns with some of their income after 1900. However, there weren't many left. This particular little book was *probably* a mid-fifteenth-century French *Book of Devotions*, measuring 4¾" x 3¼". The miniatures and borders were ascribed as the work of Phillipe de Mazerolles, Court Painter to Charles the Bold. However, Whitehouse also bought from Severn an *Office of the Virgin*, a manuscript which Ruskin called his "Salisbury Missal", and a *Book of Hours* printed in Paris by Simon Vostre between 1507 and 1527, finely illuminated by hand.

In the same letter of 22 September 1926 in which Whitehouse offered £90 for "the little book", he said: "I do hope you will send me … the drawing you have done of Ruskin's garden for the museum", to which Severn replied: "I mentioned to you my drawing

The French 15th-century *Book of Devotions* which J. H. W. bought from Arthur Severn

of Ruskin's bedroom (Brant 791) with the Turners, *not* the garden one. I could lend the garden (oil) for your museum ..." Both pictures finally came to the collection. The large oil of the path to the Professor's Garden at Brantwood (Brant 796) has only recently been positively identified as being of this subject; it was previously thought to show the gate at the end of the High Walk at Brantwood.

A short time later Severn wrote: "I will look out some drawings and send them, but am rather afraid of glass – tho' the others I sent were all right." A brief problem was created by Arthur's son Agnew, who was an executor of his mother's will and a trustee of the Ruskin Literary Trust. He had obviously remonstrated with his father over the sale of drawings and manuscripts, and on 29 September 1927 Severn wrote angrily to Whitehouse: "I was surprised to hear from my son Agnew, that he had written to tell you, that no drawings are to be sold! *All nonsense*, I am sure he is exceeding his authority as a Trustee ... Brantwood belongs to me & I have a perfect right to sell what I choose – and you of *all men* ought not to be prevented adding to your museum things I am ready to part with"; and he went on to discuss the sale of Brantwood.

Severn's painting of the approach to the Professor's Garden

Undeterred, on 2 October Severn sold to Whitehouse a mountain and lake scene by Ruskin, a watercolour of Bellinzona, a "mountain side", a map of Scotland (Brant 951) and pencil drawings of Rome, Naples, Florence (?Ponte Vecchio, Brant 911), Church Tower and Melrose (Brant 955). Whitehouse pointed out that the pencil drawings were stained (Brantwood was a *very* damp house) and Melrose was "very badly" stained, and fixed an extremely low price of £26. The drawings of Rome and Naples may well have been those which Whitehouse subsequently gave to Mussolini and the Pope. And all

John Ruskin's Map of Scotland, 1828

the time references to the proposed sale of Brantwood recur, Whitehouse having now suggested that Severn retained a life tenancy: "yes, that is what I should like". Severn replied on 24 January 1928: "if Brantwood is or may become the property of the nation – a sum of money paid to me, on account, so to speak, would be very acceptable, as I am in rather low water, with heavy debts … The chief expense at Brantwood is *coals* and *oil* – the mere carting costs about 10/- every time – apart from the coals … I had a bill the other day from co-op store at Coniston for *£63* – coals and oil."

Meanwhile, at Bembridge the school continued to grow and there was need for a new boarding house. Apart from the juniors, who had their own house in the grounds, all the seniors and the unmarried staff, including Whitehouse, lived in Yellowsands, the original house which he had bought in 1915 – and which was now called "The School House". M. H. Baillie Scott, with whom Whitehouse had done business when M.P. for Mid-Lanark, drew up plans for a building constructed around a hollow square, one side to be a home for Whitehouse and the other to be for boys' accommodation. Work began in September 1925; there were many delays and the house was not ready for occupation until the autumn term of 1927. To differentiate between the two buildings, the 1927 house became "The New School House", and the original one "The Old School House" – the names eventually being corrupted to New House and Old House. Warden moved into his wing of New House and much of his collection would have moved down the drive with him, his six rooms and two corridors giving much needed wall space for the growing picture collection.

It was at about this time that Whitehouse began to do business with the firm of B. F. Stevens & Brown Ltd, library, literary and fine-art agents. Their offices were at 4 Trafalgar Square, but around the end of 1930 they moved to fresh premises at the appropriately named "New Ruskin House", 28–30 Little Russell Street. Whitehouse almost always dealt personally with Ralph Brown, who over the next 30 years was to serve the collection well. He executed Whitehouse's saleroom commissions, and frequently drew to his

The New House at Bembridge. Whitehouse's wing is in the centre and the Galleries to the right

Ralph Brown, who acted as J. H. W.'s agent for a quarter of a century, photographed in the 1950s

attention items that Whitehouse had overlooked in catalogues or exhibitions. Whitehouse often appeared to give Brown a free hand when buying, but Brown knew his limit was very low. The two men never seem to have had a serious disagreement, despite the fact that Whitehouse would beat down the price – and the commission – to rock bottom and often kept Brown waiting for months, or even years, for settlement of his accounts.

It appears that the first commissions carried out for Whitehouse were at Christie's on 22 April 1927, where Brown bought a drawing by Ruskin of Rheinfelden for 4 guineas and a view of Coniston Water by Arthur Severn for 10 guineas (?Bem 508). From the Mrs John Lane sale on 7 July 1927 came the Samuel Laurence portrait of Ruskin for 10 guineas (Bem 305). A couple of pictures by Eleanor Fortescue Brickdale – Gather ye Rosebuds (Bem 122) and Today for me (Bem 123) – were followed at the end of 1927 or the beginning of 1928 by the purchase of several groups of letters – a series of 21 at Sotheby's in December, 23 and a "parcel" at Christie's on 21 May 1928 and four to Samuel Laurence at Puttick's on 2 July 1928. The letters in these unspecified purchases are almost certainly the groups addressed to the members of the Scott family, and those to Dr and Mrs Barnard, that Whitehouse published along with the Laurence letters in his *The Solitary Warrior* in 1929. The illustrations to this book also serve to pinpoint the purchase of further

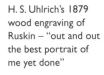

H. S. Uhlrich's 1879 wood engraving of Ruskin – "out and out the best portrait of me yet done"

Ruskin drawings which thus must have been at Bembridge before 1929. They are the Tower at Fribourg (Brant 917), the 1835 drawing of the Great Square at Bienne (Bem 1152), River and Buildings at Bremgarten in 1860 (Bem 1173), another 1835 drawing, La Residence, Munich (Brant 960), and a drawing of the Ducal Palace capital number 36 (Bem 1601). The Samuel Laurence portrait of Ruskin formed the frontispiece to the book.

Ralph Brown made an intriguing purchase for Whitehouse at Sotheby's on 31 July 1929. The invoice reads "Drawing by Sir John Millais P.R.A. 'Portrait of John Ruskin' 1879". I am at a loss to know what this £8 lot was – certainly not the Millais portrait of Ruskin (Bem 356) we now have, which was not bought until 1951. Could it have been a print of the Uhlrich wood engraving which was published in 1879?

Whitehouse admired the work of Albert Goodwin, who came under Ruskin's influence as a young man; he was with him during his illness at Matlock in 1871, and later did work for him in Oxfordshire. In the following year, with Arthur Severn, he was in the party which travelled to Italy with Ruskin. Whitehouse built up a substantial collection of watercolours and paintings by Goodwin, buying at least 20 lots (at least 25 pictures) at the Matthew Biggar Walker Sale at Christie's on 9 March 1928.

1929 was of great significance in the history of the collection, because that year saw the building of its new permanent home. "The Museum of St George", as the Ruskin Galleries were originally known, was built as an extension to Whitehouse's wing of the New House. The galleries comprise a hall with its own access onto the outside terrace or by an internal door to the rest of the house. The room on the ground floor was planned as a library, while the upstairs room was intended to be a picture gallery; both rooms were well furnished to provide not only a home for the collection, but also to engender in boys of the school, who visited the galleries for various purposes, a love of craftsmanship and art and an appreciation of quality in both – by coming into incidental contact with them rather than by having craftsmanship and art thrust upon them.

The galleries were built by Daniel Day, a builder from neighbouring Ventnor, and were designed by him in conjunction with

The Lower Gallery in the 1930s

The Upper Gallery in the 1930s

Whitehouse. They were formally opened on 19 November 1930 by Albert Rutherston, the Ruskin Drawing Master at Oxford from 1929 to 1949. Speaking at the opening ceremony, he said:

> your Warden has been inspired by far greater ideals than merely building these rooms. These rooms are the outcome of a life-long love of things spiritual and things belonging to the arts. He began to collect the contents of these rooms many years ago, and when the occasion comes, they are furnished in a manner worthy of their architecture. That spirit is a very rare spirit. It is only he who really cares and loves, who is content to build slowly and surely.

In a photograph of the gallery interior taken soon after it was built we can recognise other pictures by now in the collection. Here is the Severn oil of the path to the Professor's Garden, two oils by T. M. Rooke – of Coutances (Brant 772) and Rouen (Brant 774) – and three watercolours by him. There are two designs by Charles Fairfax Murray, Isabella Jay's copy of the Burial of Sir David Wilkie (Brant 737), and one of Ruskin's big lecture diagrams, the study of a peacock's and a falcon's feathers (Brant 907).

The collection was established in its new home – but only just in time!

CHAPTER V

SALES

The Ruskin Galleries had been opened just in time. The next few years were to see a great expansion of the collection, and the additional space provided by the two new rooms was needed.

In 1930 the Ruskin Literary Trustees, "with the Consent of Arthur Severn Esq.", took the decision to begin the formal dispersal of the contents of Brantwood. Whitehouse had, of course, been buying from Arthur Severn for several years. Almost certainly unknown to Whitehouse, the Japanese collector Ryuzo Mikimoto had made several visits to this country and to Brantwood to buy Ruskin material for *his* Ruskin collection; and possibly unknown to Arthur Severn, various visitors to Brantwood had bought from Violet Severn and the Wilkinson family.

Brantwood was now in a sorry state. After Joan Severn's death, Arthur spent most of his time in London, really only visiting Brantwood to treat it as a gold mine. Of their children, Lily had died in 1920, Agnew died in 1929 but had not lived in Brantwood for some years, Herbert had emigrated to Canada, and young Arthur had moved to Bibury in Gloucestershire, where he was interested in little but the breeding of fish. This left Violet in glorious isolation, and not entirely of this world, at Brantwood, with the Wilkinsons in the lodge to look after her, the house and estate. Visitors to the house at this time have left records of peeling wallpaper and buckets to catch rainwater dripping from two floors above. Not surprisingly, many of the pictures at Brantwood were badly stained.

Sotheby's were instructed and on Thursday 24 July 1930 a sale was held of "The Manuscripts and Remaining Library of John Ruskin". It began with 23 lots of books, including four manuscripts (three medieval and one Ruskin). Here the Greek fifteenth-century *Septuagint* brought the highest price, at £145. Stevens & Brown bought the 48 volumes of Curtis's *Botanical Magazine*, but do not appear to have offered it to Whitehouse. The 59 lots of Kate Greenaway material which followed were the most sought-after in the early part of the sale. There were *Almanacks* inscribed to Ruskin, her usual large birthday and New Year drawings for him, but the most expensive item here, bought by Maggs for £420, was a lot of 250 letters from her to Ruskin, many of them containing her little drawings.

Then followed 25 lots of books and manuscripts in which White-house took an interest. He had been able to go to the sale himself and he bought two incunabula – Gregorius Magnus, *Dialogi*, 1478, and Hyginus, *Poetica astronomica*, 1485 – the first book in which the constellations are shown as the signs of the zodiac – and a sixteenth-century Italian manuscript, *Regula della scola del sanctissimo corpo de d. iesu.*, with a large miniature on the first page. He also bought first editions of Scott's *Monastery, Peveril of the Peak, Fortunes of Nigel, Redgauntlet, Woodstock* and *Anne of Geierstein* (two lots, 19 volumes, some annotated by Ruskin, £5).

The Ruskin manuscripts followed. A large number of Ruskin's letters to his father, bound in six blue morocco volumes, fell to "Allen" for £520 and are now at Yale. The 27 "Holograph Diaries and Notebooks" which formed the next lot – lot 111 – were bought by Whitehouse for £1,600, to form what he considered to be the centrepiece of his collection. But bad selection from Brantwood and lotting on behalf of Sotheby's meant that he hadn't bought the *whole* diary, and there are still fugitive volumes in other collections.

The diary of the 1830 tour to the Lake District, once classified by Collingwood as "Juvenilia No. X", had subsequently been bound, probably at the instigation of Wedderburn. Here, then, are two reasons why it was probably housed in a different place at Brant-wood to the other diaries. Another fugitive volume is that now known as "The Brantwood Diary". This is a volume which Ruskin used only at Brantwood, between 1876 and 1883; unlike his other diaries, this volume did not travel with him, so it is a peculiarly Brantwood item. Both of these volumes have more Lake District interest than the remaining diary and were probably bought privately from Brantwood *before* the sales by the Grasmere antique dealer T. H. Telford, from whom they were both bought by F. J. Sharp. Both are now in the Pierpont Morgan Library in New York.

The third volume which escaped from lot 111 was a volume originally begun by Ruskin's father (Bem MS 18). This appeared as part of a lot in a Ruskin sale in the next year. Whitehouse objected;

the lot was withdrawn and the missing volume eventually joined the other diaries at Bembridge.

Of course, some of the confusion with the diaries is that they contain a great deal *more* than purely chronological entries; in fact some are almost entirely note-book, with hardly *any* diary entries. To add to the confusion, several different numbers or names have been assigned to the volumes – by Ruskin, Cook and Wedderburn, and Sotheby's, for example. In an attempt to clarify the position, I tabulate the information as an appendix.

After the diaries, Whitehouse allowed the next three lots to go, before bidding successfully on "Lot 115 *Stones of Venice*, 1849–51. Five cloth slip cases containing the original material". This lot, which fell to him at £440, now forms a very significant part of the collection, because it represents a high proportion of the working notes and sketches which Ruskin distilled into *The Stones of Venice*. When these are put together with material already in the collection, or to join it later, one can see exactly how Ruskin worked on the preparation of the book.

Two of the slip-cases contain eight small note-books, named by Ruskin *House Book 1, House Book 2, Gothic Book, St M[ark's] Book, Bit Book, Palace Book, Door Book, N Book 1849* (Bem 1614–1621). The remaining three larger slip-cases contained upwards of 250 sketches, plans, diagrams and so on, many of them mounted on card by Ruskin for ease of use. Many of these are numbered and dated and are now known as the "Worksheets".

J. H. W.'s purchases at the 1930 Ruskin sale – Ruskin's diaries, *Stones of Venice* working papers, a group of Ruskin's literary manuscripts, two incunabula, a medieval manuscript, and a set of Scott's novels

Facing page:
Stones of Venice Note-books – "Gothic Book", with notes on Fondaco di Turchi

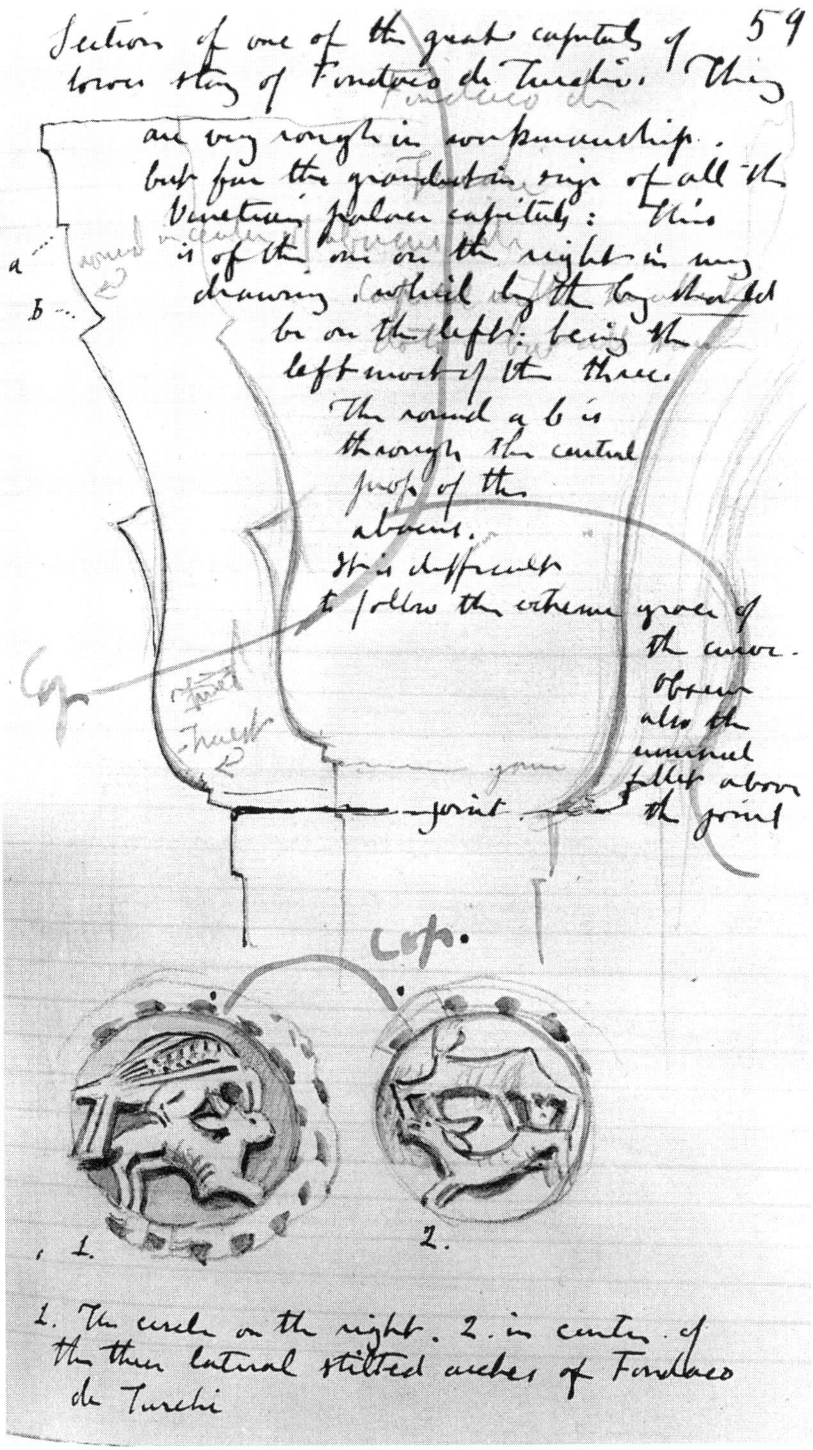

Section of one of the great capitals of lower story of Fondaco de Turchi. They are very rough in workmanship but far the grandest in size of all the Venetian palace capitals: This is of the one on the right in my drawing which by the bye should be on the left, being the left-most of the three.

The round a b is through the central part of the abacus.

It is difficult to follow the extreme grace of the curve. Observe also the unusual fillet above the joint

joint

59

a
b

1.

2.

1. The circle on the right. 2. in center of the three lateral stilted arches of Fondaco de Turchi

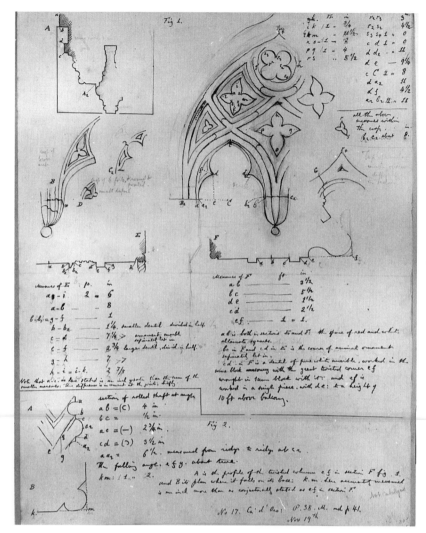

Stones of Venice Worksheet No 17, Ca' d'Oro

The note-books, the worksheets – and two other larger note-books – all need to be used in conjunction; happily, one of the other larger note-books was in lot 111, the volume now numbered 10 and known by Ruskin as "M", so that is also now at Bembridge (Bem MS 10). The outstanding volume was not classified as a diary. It is called "M2"; it was sold separately and is now in the Beinecke Library at Yale.

In the catalogue to the 1978 *Ruskin and Venice* exhibition held at the J. B. Speed Art Museum in Louisville, Robert Hewison has explained how the various components in the jigsaw work. Ruskin's daily practice, Hewison explains, was to make notes and rough sketches on the spot on the large worksheets. Ruskin had begun this method in Verona, on his way to Venice in 1849; the first Venetian worksheet was number 8, and the series continues through to number 174, when Ruskin left Venice in 1850. Number 175 is Verona again, and the sheets end with 195 at Bourges Cathedral in France. Ruskin subsequently cut up some of the sheets, and the sequence has been dispersed through several collections, but a reconstruction is still possible. It is also probable that Ruskin used the system again to a limited extent in 1851; a worksheet numbered 200 is in the collection of the Victoria and Albert Museum.

Having made his notes on the spot, Ruskin later – presumably in the evenings – wrote them up in his large note-books, M or M2. M2 was originally intended for historical as opposed to architectural notes, but at some stage Ruskin confused the two books, so that notes from the worksheets appear in both volumes. Eventually M became filled up anyway. When Ruskin had finished writing up his notes, he would write on the sheet a cross-reference to the page in the note-book. Thus "No 17 Ca' d'Oro; P. 38 M and p. 41 Nove 19th" means that this is worksheet number 17, the subject is the Ca' d'Oro, and his notes are to be found on pages 38 and 41 of note-book M; the drawing was done on 19 November 1849. The notes in M are similarly headed with the relevant worksheet number. Because of the numbered sequence and note-book M, it is possible to identify every surviving drawing and to calculate how much material is missing.

The third stage of Ruskin's studies involved the small note-books. It gradually became clear that it was useful to gather material relating to specific themes in one place. Ruskin therefore began using small note-books which fitted easily into the pocket. The system evolved gradually, and these note-books came into play one by one throughout the visit. It is possible to tell when they came into use by reference to M, which acted, as it were, as the master note-book to the series. *House Book 1* was prepared in advance, with the pages laid out by Effie Ruskin in categories for the architectural elements Ruskin was interested in. The *Door Book* is a derivation of *House Book 1*, for he found that he did not have enough room to note all the details of the doors in the space Effie had left.

Stones of Venice "M Book", notes on Fondaco di Turchi

At a later stage, probably when Ruskin had returned to England in 1850, he made a careful collation of all his Venetian note-books and wrote it up in M2. This would be a useful and rapid way to refer to specific notes when he came to write *The Stones of Venice*. In all, the system shows the care with which Ruskin approached his research. When Kenneth Clark said that, if Venice were to be destroyed, it would almost be possible to rebuild it from Ruskin's notes, sketches and measurements, he was not exaggerating *too* much! *The Stones of Venice* working papers were a very important addition to the collection.

The final lot in the sale that Whitehouse bought – for £22 – was lot 119, a miscellaneous gathering of literary manuscript fragments. Some of the fragments in this lot had been offered, and withdrawn, in the 1921 sale to which I have already referred. Also included in lot 119, but not offered in 1921, were 38 leaves of the 1878 Turner Catalogue (Bem MS 50/I), 42 leaves of *The Art of England* (Bem MS 51/E), 22 leaves of *Mornings in Florence* (now part of Bem MS 47), part of the manuscript of *Love's Meinie* (Bem MS 50/N) and 18 pages of the epilogue to *Letters on the Lord's Prayer* (Bem MS 51/M). At the end of the day Whitehouse had spent £2,089 and had assured his collection its position at the head of Ruskin collections.

1931 was to prove another very busy year for Whitehouse. Bembridge School continued to run successfully and at the beginning of the year he addressed his Society for Research in Education on "The Fagging System in English Schools and Ideals of Service". One of the principles on which Bembridge had been founded was that there was no fagging in the school and there was always an emphasis on service to others. On the following day he attended the annual London dinner of the Old Bembridgians Association, of which he was president, and on the next day he left for a visit to Rome. On 2 March he attended the opening by Sir Michael Sadler, Master of University College, of an exhibition in Oxford of 50 Ruskin drawings which he had loaned from Bembridge. Back at Bembridge on 6 March he entertained the whole school to dinner to meet Miss Margaret Chubb, to whom he had just become engaged. Their wedding took place at St Margaret's, Westminster, on 8 April, the ceremony being conducted by Dr W. R. Inge, Dean of St Paul's, after whom one of the Bembridge School sports houses had been named.

In connection with the work of the Committee for the Preservation of the *Fram*, Whitehouse was in Oslo for three days at the beginning of June, and on 20 June he was in Frankfurt with Colin Rocke, a school prefect, who had been invited to give a radio talk there describing his school life.

At Bembridge, plans were afoot for the building of a school chapel and, more immediately, work was in progress on the erection of a building to form a permanent home for the Yellowsands Press. With the emphasis which Whitehouse placed on the importance of creative education at Bembridge, he included the teaching of art, woodwork and printing on the timetable from the foundation of the school. In fact, the Yellowsands Press, as the school press is called, was originally established in Whitehouse's house in Hammersmith Terrace, London. On the advice of Emery Walker, he had bought an 1830s Albion press and with considerable difficulty this was moved into a room of Whitehouse's London home. Here, he and Edward Daws, who taught printing for the first term or two, taught themselves the "Black Art". At Bembridge the press had always been housed in unsuitable temporary accommodation until 1931, when it moved into its custom-built home – which it was to continue to occupy until the summer of 1988.

Later in the year Whitehouse contested the parliamentary constituency of Thornbury in Gloucestershire for the election on 27 October, and he also found time to write or edit two books, *The Paradise of Tintoretto* and *A Formroom Fellowship*. Meanwhile, in London, Arthur Severn died at the age of 89, on 23 February 1931. His funeral service was held at his local church, St Gabriel's, Warwick Square, S.W., and was conducted by Bishop Wild, a distant relation by marriage. Later he was buried at Coniston.

The scope of the dispersal which had begun with the 1930 sale at Sotheby's was now widened; almost everything was for sale. Sotheby's began in earnest with a silver sale on 29 April 1931, which included both Severn and Ruskin pieces, but Whitehouse was not a buyer. A miscellaneous sale on the next day included several lots that did not interest him either – J. M. W. Turner's ring, a christening cup presented by Wordsworth to one of Arthur Severn's brothers, and other trinkets. Other items were included in a sale on 8 May. Lot 49 was Ruskin's christening robe, which attracted no bid, but which came to the collection at Brantwood as a gift a few years ago. Also included in this sale were Ruskin's armchair (lot 87) and a double-sided library cupboard, each side fitted with four drawers with cupboards below to take picture frames; it stood in the centre of the study floor. Whitehouse probably acquired these pieces in 1931; certainly they are now in the collection.

The Brantwood study today. Ruskin's armchair is in the background and the double-sided library cupboard is in the centre of the floor. The bookcase in the background is one of the pair retained by Violet Severn, while the pair to the left came from the Sharp Collection

The first sale of importance in 1931 to interest Whitehouse was of "The Final Portion of the Manuscripts & Library of John Ruskin", held at Sotheby's on 18 May. Lot 12, a copy of Samuel Rogers's poem *Italy*, bound in blue velvet and inscribed to Ruskin by the author, and by Ruskin to Joan Severn, seems to have been knocked down to Whitehouse for £2 15s., but there is no trace of it in the collection now. The lot containing the diary volume for 1871–3 was withdrawn, as has already been mentioned, and that volume eventually joined the other volumes of the diary at Bembridge.

One of Whitehouse's most important additions to the collection was lot 33 in this sale, which he secured for a modest £6. The lot is described as "Correspondence with Miss Joanna Agnew, afterwards Mrs Arthur Severn, many hundreds of ALS 1864–1888, also a large number of his correspondent's answers" (Bem L 33–62). Sotheby's description of the lot was rather modest; it comprised about 3,020 letters from Ruskin to Joan written between 1864 and 1895, and about 650 of her letters dated between 1867 and 1899. Biographically, this is probably the most important series of Ruskin letters in existence. Ruskin wrote to Joan almost every day – and sometimes

even more than once a day – when they were apart, and in the letters
he tells her all he is doing. From this point of view, they are far more
important than the diaries; however, they do also contain working
notes and material. On more than one occasion when he was abroad
Ruskin numbered the pages of the *series* of letters consecutively,
telling Joan to keep them safe because he was writing to her rather
than in his diary. Here we can trace where he was on almost any day
of his life after the death of his father; we know where he stayed –
often what he ate – who he corresponded with, who he spoke to,
what he saw and what he did. When he was at Brantwood and Joan
was in London, we learn of the progress in the house. When he was
at Oxford, we hear of the reception of his lectures. The purchase
of this lot was certainly one of Whitehouse's most significant
achievements.

Substantially the correspondence is complete, although there *are*
a few gaps. A group of 26 letters from the Continent dated between
12 September and 30 October 1888 is in the University of Illinois
Library, and the three long letters of the "Christmas Story" and an
allied group of letters to Joan passed from the Sharp collection to
Helen Viljoen and on to the Pierpont Morgan Library.

Really, it is surprising that there are not larger gaps in the
correspondence. It was examined by Wedderburn, who used
extracts from many of the letters for the introductions to the *Library
Edition* volumes and the two volumes of letters. He, of course, was
selective, in that he did not use anything that would show Ruskin in
what he or Joan Severn would have considered a bad light. But
before Wedderburn's arrival at Brantwood to consult material, Sara
Anderson would already have been through the letters to remove
anything that "Alec need not see" – and before that Joan herself had
removed other letters! So the survival of almost the entire correspondence is remarkable. Each annual (or smaller) group of letters
was carefully wrapped in paper by Sara Anderson – Ruskin's secretary and later Kipling's, described by Sidney Cockerell as "a sort of
super-secretary" – and endorsed by her on the outside with details
of the contents of the packet. When I came to catalogue the manuscripts of the Bembridge collection some 30 years after the letters
were bought, they were still in Sara Anderson's wrapping, and
parcelled up as they had come here from Sotheby's. If Whitehouse
had opened any of the packets, he hadn't opened many!

For £4 Whitehouse picked up a letter from Robert Browning to Ruskin (lot 34; Bem L 7). His next bid was for lot 40A, uncatalogued, a group of 49 letters from Ruskin's father to Mrs Simon, and this bid was successful at £2 15s. (Bem L 12). Mrs Simon's husband John was a doctor by profession, and has been described as "the greatest of Victorian civil servants". Simon was responsible for setting up the Medical Officership of Health in London. Later he built up the new Medical Department of State and was the government's first medical adviser. The Simon family and the Ruskin family were friends of long standing; John Simon advised both Mr and Mrs Ruskin on health matters in their old age, and years later he attended Ruskin in his illnesses. Interestingly, this uncatalogued lot of letters also included three photographs (presumably of Ruskin) and "a pen and ink drawing of John Ruskin". This drawing may well be the pen and ink self-portrait of about 1860 which is now Bem 1507. There does not seem to be any reference to it in the correspondence, but the Simons were frequently at Denmark Hill and it may have been given to them on one of these visits.

John Ruskin's self-portrait, c. 1860

Whitehouse's interest fell next on lots 41–43. Here was a parcel of 265 letters from Ruskin's father to his son (Bem L 3–4), 80 from his father to his mother (Bem L 2) and 154 letters from Margaret Ruskin to her husband (Bem L 1). Sandwiched between these two lots of letters was a group of volumes, again of great biographical importance – John James Ruskin's diary, 1852–64 (Bem MS 33), his 1838–42 letter book (Bem MS 34) and two volumes of his personal account books from 1827 to 1864 (Bem MS 28–29). The diary contains summaries of some of his correspondence with John and lists of dinner guests, together with lists of friends to whom he gave copies of his son's books. His account books form an almost complete record of every penny he spent in the final 37 years of his life – on his son's education, his own and his wife's clothes, his household accounts, his cellar, his charities, his travels (curiously, always linked with his medical expenses!) and, perhaps most importantly, his picture collection.

Another group of printed books followed the manuscripts in the sale, with Whitehouse picking up Forbes's *Travels through the Alps*, 1845, Sir Herbert Edwardes's *A Year on the Punjab Frontier*, 2 vols,

The Lower Gallery, or Warden's Library, today. The cases to the left of the fireplace now contain some of the books formerly in Ruskin's library, and the "Mikimoto Gift"

1851, and half a dozen more (lot 77, £1 10s.) and Gibbon's *Decline and Fall of the Roman Empire*, 12 vols, 1838 (lot 78, 5 guineas) – all of them annotated by Ruskin.

It must have given Whitehouse particular pleasure to buy lot 113, although he had to pay £36 for it, for this was the illuminated address of congratulation that he had taken to Brantwood to present to Ruskin in 1899, completed now and preserved in its red morocco box (Bem MS 81). Completed, yes – but by now the central folio of the manuscript, containing the section devoted to the Royal Academy of Arts and the Royal Institute of British Architects, had been removed and given to the Coniston Museum, where it may still be seen.

The last in the series of Ruskin sales at Sotheby's was held on 20 May 1931. This dispersed "The Collection of Pictures and Drawings", and was of particular interest to Whitehouse, who perhaps delighted particularly in Ruskin's drawings. Again, he was able to attend the sale himself and his marked copy of the catalogue records what he bought. The first lot which fell to him, for £5, was a group of six landscapes and architectural watercolours by Ruskin's secretary and friend W. G. Collingwood. In the absence of additional information, it is not possible to determine *which* drawings were in this lot. Perhaps one of them was a watercolour which Collingwood had made of the Via Fillungo when he was in Lucca with Ruskin in 1882 – an interesting view showing the church of S. Cristoforo and the fourteenth-century Torro dell'Ore with its contemporary clock (Bem 165).

The study of the sculpture of Noah from the Vine Angle of the Ducal Palace in Venice (lot 11, £1 10s., Bem 143) is a fine example of the work of Raffaele Carloforti. Carloforti was one of the group of Venetian artists supported by Ruskin, or commissioned by him to execute work for the Guild of St George. Although we know that he copied some paintings for Ruskin, the only examples of his work which seem to have survived are studies of sculpture. The guild collection has a fine study of the head of S. Simeon in S. Simeone Grande, Venice, commissioned by Ruskin in 1876, and a study of birds and grapes from the Vine Angle which dates from the same time. No doubt this study of Noah formed part of the same commission, but having reached Brantwood, it was retained by Ruskin and never sent to Sheffield.

A study of Noah from the Vine Angle of the Ducal Palace, Venice, by Raffaele Carloforti

A group of three watercolours by Albert Goodwin (lot 13, £5 10s.), included a nice study of the Ponte Vecchio in Florence, made in 1880 (Bem 210). Goodwin had first visited Florence in 1872 when in Italy with Ruskin, and in his memoir of Ruskin Arthur Severn noted that "Goodwin and I made careful drawings of the Ponte Vecchio and other subjects". The lot also included a view of the interior of St Mark's (Brant 725).

In the 1860s Ruskin's interest in Winnington Hall, a girls' school in Cheshire, and the possibility of buying a home for himself in

Albert Goodwin's watercolour of the Ponte Vecchio, Florence

Switzerland, combined in the plan for Burne-Jones to design a series of wall hangings illustrating Chaucer's *Dream of Fair Women*, to be embroidered at Winnington. The plan never came to fruition because, apparently, the designs were too difficult for the girls to work. But some of the designs were completed. Thisbe from the series is now in the William Morris Gallery at Walthamstow. The large study of Chaucer dreaming of the fair women, which was to have been the centrepiece of the series, was at Brantwood (lot 17) and Whitehouse bought it for £19 (Bem 132).

There were several other lots of Burne-Jones watercolours or drawings in the sale, for which he did not bid. One miscellaneous lot (lot 21) included "Two designs for Kings' Pleasures and Queens' Gardens". These were drawings which Burne-Jones made for Ruskin's projected editions of books which were never issued. Although he did not bid on this lot in the sale, Whitehouse was later to buy the two designs.

Ambrogio Lorenzetti's frescoes on three of the walls of the Sala del Pace in the Palazzo Pubblico in Siena were painted between 1337 and 1340. That part of the series known as The Policy of Siena was copied for Ruskin by another artist, Charles Fairfax Murray, in 1873. Murray was commissioned by Ruskin to make a series of copies of paintings in Italy for the Guild of St George, and it is possible that,

Chaucer, by Edward Burne-Jones

like the Carloforti Noah, the Murray Policy of Siena (lot 25, 5 guineas, Bem 375) was intended for Sheffield. Whatever the original intention, Whitehouse added the picture to his collection.

Charles Fairfax Murray's study of Lorenzetti's Policy of Siena

W. G. Collingwood: John Ruskin in his Brantwood study, 1897

John Ruskin: Dover Castle, 1832

John Ruskin: Hôtel de ville, Cassel, 1833

John Ruskin: Mount Pilatus, pencil study, 1835

John Ruskin: Mount Pilatus, watercolour, 1835

John Ruskin: Street in St Gall, pencil, 1835

John Ruskin: Street in St Gall, ink, 1835

John Ruskin: Peterborough Cathedral,
1837

John Ruskin: Rosslyn Chapel, 1838

John Ruskin: Trevi Fountain, Rome, 1840–41

John Ruskin: Street scene in Naples, 1841

John Ruskin: Bridge at Terni, 1841

John Ruskin: Square at Cologne, 1842

John Ruskin: Mountain rock and alpine rose, 1844

John Ruskin: Visp, c. 1844

John Ruskin: Rothhorn and Arrêt Blanche, 1845

John Ruskin: Fruit and vegetable gondola, 1845

Facing page:
John Ruskin: Palazzo Minischalchi, Verona, 1845

John Ruskin: Casa d'Oro, Venice, 1845

Palazzo Minischalchi
VERONA.

John Ruskin: Mount Pilatus, 1846

Facing page:
John Ruskin: Palazzo Dario, Venice, c. 1846

John Ruskin: Tree study, perhaps at Ambleside, 1847

John Ruskin: Byzantine ruin, Rio di Ca' Foscari – stilted archivolts, Venice, 1849

John Ruskin: Mer de Glace, 1849

Daguerreotype: Mer de Glace

John Ruskin: Summit of Mont Blanc, 1851

Lot 105 contained four watercolours by Arthur Severn, The Salute, Venice (Brant 798), Sunset at Mullion, Cornwall (Bem 523) and Clouds at San Giorgio, Venice (Brant 788). The largest drawing in the lot is probably the least attractive, Gulls at Ravenglass (Bem 531). The four came to Whitehouse for £3 5s. He also bought three miscellaneous lots (121, £10; 136, £3 10s.; 146, £2 10s.) which included work by J. W. Bunney, T. M. Rooke, Frank Randal, Francesca Alexander, Emily Warren, H. Stacy Marks, Mrs La Touche (Cloissoné vase; Bem 304), J. W. Whymper (Rosslyn Chapel, 1858; Bem 623) and Angelo Alessandri (interior of St Mark's, 1903; Brant 702).

The one oil painting bought at the sale (lot 135, £9; Bem 551) was catalogued by Sotheby's as sixteenth-century Venetian, "The Virgin and Child with St Catherine offering flowers". Although this was shown in the catalogue as having belonged to Arthur Severn and as coming from Warwick Square, it almost certainly was originally Ruskin's.

The greatest number of pictures in the sale were, of course, by Ruskin himself. Many of these lots comprised more than one picture. Whitehouse was successful in buying 20 lots; for a total of £131 5s. he acquired 51 drawings. In some cases, it is difficult to decide *which* is the picture actually described in the lot, but among the more important identifiable drawings were several early examples; in one lot (81, £3 10s.) was the 1832 pencil study of Richmond Hill (Bem 1458), inscribed to show that it was one of Ruskin's first studies from nature, a significant drawing, and the pencil study of the Hôtel de Ville, Cassel (Bem 1198), dating from the 1833 continental tour and the first drawing made by Ruskin on the Continent. Lot 56 (£2 10s.) contained some even earlier drawings, some of Ruskin's early copies of maps – "My first map of Italy", 1827 (Bem 1384), North America, c. 1828 (Brant 950), Spain and Portugal, c. 1828 (Brant 952), Historical Map of France, 1884 (Brant 949), and the Physical Geography of Palestine (Bem 1385).

There was a view of the Tyrolese mountains from Munich, 1852 (lot 52, £7, Brant 1021), two pencil sketches of Neuchâtel (lot 60, £1; Brant 964, 965), studies of sculpture at Chartres (lot 80, £1 5s.; Brant 897) and Amiens, Florence and Venice (lot 74, £1). Other studies in Italy included a pencil drawing of the Ponte di Trinita, Florence (lot 59, £4 15s.; Bem 1256) with a drawing of Siena, and the large watercolour and body colour drawing of the upper part of the tomb of Can Signorio della Scala in Verona (lot 41, £2 10s.; Bem 1667). In fact, at this sale Whitehouse was able to buy most of Ruskin's largest drawings – he secured the 4ft x 3ft drawing of the Castelbarco Tomb in Verona, 1869 (Brant 1071; lot 46, £4, where it was inaccurately described as "The Scaliger Tombs, Verona").

Amazingly, the large and supremely important architectural study, the north-west porch of St Mark's, 1877 (Bem 1633), was lotted with another large drawing, the study of Zipporah from Botticelli's Life of Moses (Brant 880). Whitehouse secured the two for £41 – by far his highest bid in the sale.

The drawing of the north-west porch of St Mark's is possibly Ruskin's most beautiful and successful architectural study. In Ruskin's time, it was one of the small number of his own drawings to be hung at Brantwood, and it occupied a key position above the shell cabinet on the end wall of the drawing-room – where it is still usually to be seen. It is a much-exhibited drawing, and it was copied by Ruskin so that he could send the copy, rather than the original, across the Atlantic to C. E. Norton's exhibition of Ruskin drawings at Boston in 1879. The study of Zipporah from the fresco in the Sistine Chapel was one of the largest Old Master studies made by Ruskin. It is still in its original frame. It too hung – and still hangs – in the Brantwood drawing-room, adjacent to the shell cabinet. Secured in the same sale (lot 91) was Ruskin's copy of Zipporah's Flock, 1874 (Brant 879), from the same fresco. This came in the same lot, for a modest £2, as "King David (after Tintoretto)" – in fact, probably Angelo Alessandri's study of King David (Bem 9) – the study of the chair, from Carpaccio's St Jerome, in his study, 1876 (Brant 889), an initial from an Irish manuscript (perhaps Brant 935) and a detail from a picture by an Italian Old Master.

Another £2 bid (lot 83) secured two 1874 studies of frescoes in the Spanish Chapel in Florence, Astronomy and Music (Brant 914) and Grammar (Brant 915) and The Triumph of the Dominican Order – a small watercolour sketch of The Church Militant fresco in the Spanish Chapel (Brant 916). And for good measure the lot also included the watercolour of St Martin's, opposite Sallenches.

More Old Master studies were included in lot 84 for £5. Here were the two studies after Veronese's Cucchina Family, the study of the family (Bem 1669) and the detail of the boy's head (Bem 1670),

Ruskin's large study of the Castelbarco Tomb, Verona, 1869

both made in 1859. The same lot also included a study after Luini in Milan (Brant 945) and Boats at Venice (Brant 1054). The final picture in this lot was described as a watercolour of The Visitation after Tintoretto. There is no drawing of this title in the collection now, and its identification is in doubt.

Other drawings after Tintoretto were the study of The Crucifixion, 1845 (Bem 1553), a drawing in lamp black and wash which has been in at least a dozen exhibitions, and another of Ruskin's

A study by Ruskin after Luini

largest works, the big study of the Adoration (Bem 1551). This study from the Adoration – Ruskin was evidently interested in the composition rather than the colour, which is very different from the original painting in the Scuola S. Rocco in Venice – was made during Ruskin's stay in Venice in 1852 and he wrote to his father asking him to let Mr Foord have "a rich deep frame" ready for the drawing when Ruskin returned home with it. The framed drawing must always have hung in Ruskin's homes; it is too large to have been anywhere else. Now it occupies a special position in the Upper Gallery at Bembridge, still exhibited in its original but now very brittle frame.

This sale of 20 May 1931 was the last of the sales at Sotheby's of material removed from Brantwood and Warwick Square. Still to come were the sales on site to disperse the remaining contents. The sale at 9 Warwick Square, S.W.1, was arranged by Rogers, Chapman and Thomas, and was held on 15 and 16 July. With his otherwise busy life, it is not surprising that Whitehouse was unable to attend in person. In fact, the first day's sale was comprised almost entirely of purely household effects, although lot 296 contained the remains of a china dessert service which had belonged to Ruskin, and lot 264, which eventually found its way into the collection of the late Mr Luis Gordon, importer of Domecq sherry, was the glass from which Edward VII was reputed to have tasted sherry for the first time.

It was the second day's sale which was of interest to collectors. With the exception of lot 455, a pair of Ruskin's slippers in a bag made by Lady Stansfeld, and lot 456, Ruskin's dress suit (which was subsequently acquired from a Shepherd's Bush collector of Victoriana in 1973), all of the lots comprised books, pictures, or manuscripts. It seems likely that Whitehouse hoped to attend the second day's sale and was prevented from doing so at the last moment. So he telephoned his instructions to Ralph Brown, who represented him, and who reported at the end of the day.

New Ruskin House
July 17th 1931

Dear Sir:

Referring to your telephone message yesterday regarding the sale at 9, Warwick Square, we are sorry that we could not write to you last evening on this matter as certain circumstances occurred at the sale which made our return too late to be able to render you a satisfactory account.

The sale was very strongly attended by the book trade, but unfortunately the lots, which had been hurriedly catalogued, had been tied together in bundles the contents of which were not allowed to be disturbed during the sale to ascertain whether the Brantwood bookplate or annotations in Ruskin's hand were present, and the time was so short before the sale that in any case it would have been impossible to have examined the library conscientiously under several days' work, and the consequence was that we only made one or two purchases on your behalf between lots 328 and 441 [the lots of books] as we had to take our chance as to whether the bookplates or signatures were in the books, and therefore until we have cleared the goods and examined the contents of the various lots we shall not be able to give you a full report. The vast majority of the books were purchases by one of our friends in the book-trade, who, we have since learned, catalogued the items, and we have arranged with him to make a full perusal of his purchases and afterwards we will report to you any interesting items which come within the sphere of your requirements. We do not think his prices would be excessive, but as to that we cannot tell for a week or so, meanwhile anything we have purchased with direct Ruskin or Severn associations which has not been earmarked or commissioned elsewhere we shall be sending to you in due course.

Generally speaking the prices were low but being guided by your implied limit of one pound a lot, we did not spend much on the books. We did not get the letters which were placed together in one lot and realised the sum of £90 [398 letters, 1866–71, from Ruskin to his mother, originally catalogued as lots 446–452].

Regarding the oil paintings by Mr Arthur Severn, Miss Horne was present and appeared to be buying every lot on her own behalf, purchasing at prices varying from 2½ to 8 guineas, we being the underbidders on every desirable item, but when the last, and to our mind, one of the best, oil paintings was placed on the easel, we felt it incumbent upon us to make at least one purchase for you; this was lot 481 which appears from the label at the back to be the picture entitled "Cloud effects near the Lizard" which was exhibited at the Institute of Painters in Oil Colours, and we purchased it for 9½ guineas, (by kind permission of Miss Horne), who, we afterwards learned intended to protect the sale of the Arthur Severn pictures.

[Miss M. L. Horne was an ardent admirer of Arthur Severn. She was apparently involved in the cataloguing of the sale and she wrote the foreword to the catalogue. In a pencil note appended to the foreword in Whitehouse's copy, Miss Horne wrote: "He was never at a loss of finding beautiful effects, of such beauty which are the outcome only of elevated thoughts & a love of beauty and Truth pursued with absolute & never varying sincerity".]

Since there was no opposition we bought all the Ruskin drawings [lots 484–492, containing 17 drawings] at ridiculously low prices and when we have cleared and sorted these out we will write to you again, since we feel that a little research work will reveal the importance of some of the purchases, but as promised on the telephone we will pass on to you any items that we are free to negotiate with.

When the watercolour drawings by Arthur Severn, Lot 505 etc., were offered a minor sensation was caused in the room by the intervention of Miss Horne, and a discussion followed between the auctioneer and herself regarding the lowness of the prices being paid for the goods, with the result that she withdrew the whole of the watercolour drawings of Arthur Severn [about 70 lots] so that we were unable to purchase any further examples beyond the one oil painting referred to above. There was a nice *Walter* Severn watercolour, "Setting Sun over the Sea" Lot 586 [a large study of the sea at Biarritz, 1895; Bem 555] which we purchased for you for 24 shillings as we felt sure you would like the association, and we also bought 608 and 609 together for 18 shillings, these representing five oil paintings after the great masters by Joseph Severn. These frames are in rather poor condition and of course everything is very dirty and neglected. When we have cleared the goods and made a proper inspection would you like us to render you an estimate for putting the frames in order, or shall we send the goods unframed or just as they are?

[Joseph Severn, Arthur's father, and the friend of Keats, lived for much of his life in Rome, where he was the British Consul. He supplemented his income by painting copies of Old Masters and selling them to visitors. The catalogue descriptions were not strictly accurate. The paintings are: lot 608, Veronese, St Agata Martyr (Florence; Bem 554) and Titian, Doge Grimani Kneeling before Faith (Ducal Palace; Bem 552); lot 609, Rubens, St George and the Dragon (Brant 777), Titian, Head of St John the Baptist (Brant 778) and Head and Shoulders of a Saint (Bem 553).]

Our total expenditure on your behalf did not nearly reach the figure agreed upon so that we will look around amongst the trade for some items of Brantwood interest and inscribed copies, and notify you in due course.

We enclose herewith a copy of the catalogue of the Sale to be held at Brantwood, Coniston the week after next and if we can be of any assistance to you your instructions will have our best attention. It is probable that among the books, (Lot 653 to the end of the sale), there will be some items which will appeal to you and almost certainly bearing the Brantwood bookplate.

In this matter we are having the benefit of the assistance of our friend Mr Hugh Allen [the son of George Allen, Ruskin's publisher], and his help has been invaluable. The lack of interest shown by the Severn family in all matters pertaining to Ruskin together with the appalling condition in which things at Warwick Square were left, we feel augurs well for the chances of procuring items of interest at Brantwood at reasonable prices, providing sufficient time can be given for inspection. The goods are stated to be on view from Friday next, but if you think it advisable, we will endeavour to make arrangements for Mr Allen or one of our representatives to obtain permission to inspect the goods *privately beforehand*. The expense of this should not be very much and we feel it would be a very good plan to adopt, to our mutual advantage.

As far as we are aware this Sale is not generally known in the South since one of our directors happened to be passing through the Lake District a few weeks ago, and out of curiosity visited Brantwood with the result that we have received the enclosed catalogue at his request. Therefore perhaps the best policy will be to keep this information *more or less confidential*.

We hope we can be of service to you, and awaiting your further commands, remain,

Yours faithfully,

B. F. Stevens & Brown, Ltd.,

Ralph Brown

P.S. We are also sending a copy of the Coniston catalogue to our American customer. He may not get it in time, but we can serve you both to mutual advantage, we hope, if he does reply.

[Their American customer was the Boston bookseller and Ruskin collector, Charles Goodspeed.]

Acknowledging the letter, Whitehouse regretted that Brown hadn't bought more for him, "but I realise the special difficulties you had", and he expressed the hope that he "will pass on to me as many as possible of these items, for I very much want them for this Gallery".

Writing again on 21 July, Brown reported that he had secured six lots of books for him from Warwick Square, comprising 71 volumes, for a total of £8 11s. Some of the volumes had bookplates and annotations by Ruskin and the lots included Cuvier's *The Animal Kingdom*, 1854, David Roberts's *Holy Land*, 1855, 3 vols, Lane's *Arabian Nights Entertainments*, 1883, 3 vols, Turner's *Liber Studiorum*, 1871, 4 vols, Fuller's *Introduction to Prudence*, 1815, inscribed by Ruskin to Joan Agnew, Pharsalia's *De Bello Civili*, 1719,

The road to Florence, 1845, by Ruskin

inscribed by Ruskin's mathematics teacher "To Mr Ruskin Junr with J. Rowbotham's best respects and best wishes for his welfare and happiness", and Rose La Touche's copy of Ruskin's *Queen of the Air*, 1869, with her signature on the title page.

In the same letter Brown reported on the drawings by Ruskin which he had bought for Whitehouse. There was a watercolour of Lucerne made on 31 August, 1846 (lot 485, £3 6s.; Bem 1377), The Road to Florence, 1845 (lot 487, £2 12s. 6d.; Bem 1260), two studies of details from Tintoretto's Adoration (lot 488, 14s.; Bem 1552 and Brant 1009), a pencil drawing of Schaffhausen (Brant 990) and six others (lot 489, 5 guineas) and a pair of watercolours (lot 490, £1 12s.), one of a bridge and one of a chateau.

The dust didn't have time to settle after the Warwick Square sale before plans were being laid for the sale at Brantwood. Writing to Brown, Whitehouse said that he hoped to be at Brantwood for the first day of the sale, and possibly also for the other two days.

> I should like, however, to act in co-operation with you, and for you to buy on my behalf on all three days, if you think this would be the best plan. If, however, I am present on the Tuesday I should like first to see you in order to arrange our method of operations. I want to get all the Ruskin drawings I possibly can,

and there are a number of other things of Ruskinian interest, which I should like to get.

In the event, Whitehouse was unable to attend the sale at all, and was represented there by Brown.

The Sale of "Antique Furniture, Pictures and Drawings, Books, Silver and Electroplate, Glass, Outside Effects, and Garden Plants" was arranged by the Barrow-in-Furness auctioneers, Lowden and Postlethwaite, and was held on Tuesday, Thursday and Friday, 28, 30, and 31 July 1931 "at 11.30 p.m. [sic] each day".

The Severns' younger daughter Violet, who had lived for most of her life at Brantwood, was to move into a substantial house, No. 1 Lake Villas, in Lake Road, Coniston, taking with her whatever furniture and other Ruskin items she wished. In this way, a number of pieces of furniture have become split up and others temporarily lost to Ruskin scholarship. For example, the two bookcases which stood in the study and were called "Botany" and "Geology" originally stood on cabinet bases containing several drawers. Violet took the bookcases with her from Brantwood, but did not want the cabinets. She had stained deal bases made for them, and the cabinets remained at Brantwood. They may well have been lots 105 and 106 in the sale, "Mahogany case containing six specimen drawers … by Snell". After Violet Severn's death on 7 March 1940, Whitehouse acquired the two cabinet-less bookcases and they are now again in the Brantwood study, while the cabinets, sold at the sale in 1931, are in a private collection elsewhere in the Lake District.

Built to occupy the whole of the study wall facing the fireplace was a large sectional fitting comprising six cabinets fitted with drawers and housing Ruskin's important collection of minerals. These cabinets were topped by a bookcase. The whole was lot 94 in the catalogue and appears to be complete there. Now the cabinets are in the same Lake District collection as the bases to the other bookcases, but the bookcase top is missing. Perhaps Violet decided after the catalogue had been printed that she would retain the bookcase portion.

Among the pictures that Violet Severn took with her to Lake Villas were the 1861 and 1873 Ruskin self-portraits. These were subsequently bought from her by the Barrow-in-Furness Ruskin collector F. J. Sharp, and they are now in the Pierpont Morgan Library.

Immediately before the sale the interior of Brantwood must have looked a sorry sight. Not only had the fabric suffered from years of neglect and damp, many of the pictures and other pieces had already been removed for sale in London, much had been disposed of privately and, presumably, the furniture earmarked by Violet Severn for her own use had also been removed to a place of safety.

Some attempt had been made between the London sales and the final dispersal to keep the place looking reasonable. For example, after the removal of the della Robbia plaque from the study, its place was temporarily filled by Bonifazio's Portrait of a Venetian Nobleman, which Ruskin had bought for 16 shillings in Venice in 1852. The Bonifazio was just one of the many items which were never catalogued. Nevertheless, it was bought at the sale by a lady living near Spark Bridge, only a few miles from Brantwood. In the 1960s I had it in my bedroom for several weeks until negotiations for its purchase were pre-empted by the owner's death. I had to return the painting, and I did not know until too late that it had been sold in May 1970 to an unidentified buyer at Phillips's in London for £6.

Another item which, incredibly, slipped through the net, is the magnificent dining-table. It was not included in the catalogue, does not feature in any of the Whitehouse correspondence, but was certainly at Brantwood in 1937 (although it isn't listed in Whitehouse's *Ruskin and Brantwood* published in that year), so it could not have been retained by Violet and taken to Lake Villas. Perhaps she gave it to Whitehouse.

The Times reporter summed up the general feeling of the Brantwood sale on 4 August:

> The glory that was Brantwood fizzled out last week in circumstances that could not very well have been more depressing or pathetic … It would not be technically correct to state that the sale was, as is usual in such cases, held "on the premises", for the things were sold in the garden and for the most part in the rain, and nothing can be more depressing for an auction sale of this kind.

It is evident that Whitehouse had instructed Brown about the lots he wished to buy and, in Whitehouse's absence, Brown bought for him on the first day, telegraphing to him on the following day, Wednesday 29 July, a day when there was no sale. Brown reported:

Purchases yesterday totalled forty two pounds including drinking cup ten guineas prices erratic telegraph today if any limit total expenditure also how much for books Friday as must leave for London Thursday but have arranged for Friday's bidding.

To this, Whitehouse telegraphed his reply on the same day.

No total limit tomorrow provided each lot reasonable. Anxious to get all the drawings by Ruskin and others we marked especially Rooke lot 378. Limit for books Friday twenty pounds only annotated or signed copies wanted. Send drinking cup registered post here.

Brown followed his telegram of 29 July with a more detailed account of his activities on the first day.

Dear Sir,

Your telegrams came duly to hand at Brantwood and I am very sorry you could not attend, as there were some points on which your judgement would have been welcomed.

I have sent you a long telegram explaining position to date, and shall hope to get an answer before I leave tomorrow afternoon.

I must explain that the posts here are awful, the telephone ditto & the weather also. It has poured with rain and the auctioneer held the sale *out in the garden in the rain*. Most ridiculous & uncomfortable.

I bought the following for you

80 –	1. 10. 0
101 –	6. 10. 0 (a fine price)
104 –	1. 2. 0
126 –	3. 15. 0
251 –	2. 0. 0
254 –	5. 10. 0
256 –	10. 15. 0
264 –	10. 10. 0
	£41. 12. 0

I did not get the following as I thought prices excessive, in spite of your wish to have them. (A private collector was there.)

lot   82 – sold for £24. 0. 0.
        83 – sold for £17. 0. 0.
    225 – sold for 14/- very poor, not worth having

I bought a few things for myself which you can see when I return to London.

Regarding *Drinking Cup*. The auctioneer announced that he had sold a similar one for over *£100* – without any Ruskin association. Anyhow, it is fairly bought I think at £10/10/- & according to a north country dealer next to me quite cheap for silver alone.

The post leaves in ten minutes & so I will write later after *tomorrow*.

This letter was followed later in the day by a postcard correcting an error:

I have reported lot 101 as bought for you in error. I must let you know later about it as there seems to have been a little misunderstanding at the sale. I am at Ambleside and must post this before returning to Coniston, or post will be too late tonight. It is still pouring with rain so I think you have not missed much pleasure by remaining in the Isle of Wight!

And in response to Whitehouse's telegraphed instruction of 29 July, Brown telegraphed his reply from Coniston on the next day: "No facilities packing will mail cup from London Saturday bought all you want but prices much higher today."

The items which Brown told Whitehouse he had bought were:

lot 80   Madonna and Child, copy, possibly by Joseph Severn from an original probably by Botticelli, oil on canvas, 41" x 41" (Bem 121).

lot 101   Terrestrial globe. There are the remains of two globes now at Brantwood, given to Whitehouse in the 1940s. Brown reported this purchase in error, but it may have been one of the two 1940s gifts.

lot 104   Bust of Ruskin by Barbara Collingwood. In 1919 Collingwood's daughter Barbara sculpted a large bust of Ruskin which is now in the Coniston Museum. She also made a smaller replica from which copies were cast – of which this is one (Bem R 82).

lot 126 A pair of small bird drawings by H. Stacy Marks, a stork drawn at Amiens in 1863 (Bem 346) and a bullfinch dated 26 July 1890 (Bem 318).

lot 251 "Swiss Scene". This was identified by Brown in a later letter as the important pencil and watercolour drawing of the Mer de Glace from the Montanvert, 1849 (Bem 1206). The catalogue description indicates the size as 21" x 26"; the catalogue had in fact given the *frame* size, the drawing measuring 10⅞ x 19⅞.

lot 254 "Swiss Scene" again. This was later identified as a drawing of the Glacier des Bois. There are now four drawings of the Glacier des Bois in the collection: Bem 1205, which is a drawing made in ?1856 for *Modern Painters*, Brant 894, a more distant general view, Brant 895, a watercolour of the glacier made in 1856, and the beautiful drawing made in the early 1840s (Brant 893) in imitation of a Turner vignette, for publication in *Friendship's Offering* for 1843.

lot 256 Another drawing described as "Swiss Scene" is in fact Ruskin's 1849 Chamouni drawing of the Aiguille Charmoz, drawn from the window of the Union Hotel (Brant 892), one of Ruskin's fine mountain studies of the period.

lot 264 "Ruskin's Drinking Cup, with lid, engraved and floral ornamentation". Whitehouse clearly set great store by this piece, and I have never really understood its significance. It began life as a plain silver tankard, hall-marked 1772. An inscription on the base indicates that it was given to Ruskin by "LD". The donor is so far unidentified, and it is not known if it was in fact a christening gift, or if it was given to Ruskin by a friend later in life. Subsequently, it was either given by Ruskin to the Severns, or inherited by them. At some stage, the plain tankard was transformed into a little hot-water jug by the addition of a spout and hinged lid and the insertion of insulators into the handle; the whole was heavily decorated with repoussé work. The escutcheon on the side is engraved with the initials JAS, viz

perhaps for J [oan and] A [rthur] S [evern]. Did Ruskin give it to them at the time of the wedding or at some other anniversary?

The lots for which Brown appears to have held commissions and did *not* buy were:

lot 82   Portrait of Ruskin by W. G. Collingwood, 1897, a companion to the similar portrait in the Coniston Museum (Bem 163).

lot 83   Portrait of Doge Andrea Gritti by W. G. Collingwood, after Catena. The original painting, then thought to be by Titian, which Ruskin bought from the Rev. Gilbert Elliot, Dean of Bristol, for £1,000 in 1864 was produced at the Whistler *v* Ruskin libel action as evidence of what Ruskin considered "sound workmanship". At Brantwood, it hung over the dining-room fireplace. It was sold by the Severns in about 1918 and is now in the National Gallery, where it is attributed to Catena. Before its sale it was copied by Collingwood, and his copy replaced the original in the dining-room. At the sale it seems to have been bought by Mrs C. D. Cooper of Oak Bank Private Hotel, Bowness, who had also bought the previous lot. She eventually presented both paintings to the collection, as recorded in the 1939–40 Annual Report of the Friends of Brantwood. The Doge portrait still hangs in the Brantwood dining-room (Brant 714).

lot 225   Damningly described by Brown as "not worth having", this "Terrace" was a watercolour by Severn after Turner.

Whitehouse must have been disappointed at not securing more on the first day, and particularly sorry not to have got the two Collingwood portraits. In fact, his purchases on that day were not very impressive.

Following his return to London, in a letter dated 1 August, Brown reported to Whitehouse his progress on the second and third days of the sale:

In the second day's sale, which was far better attended and for which certain people evidently held commissions, we purchased the following:–

Lot 321 – H.S. Marks drawing [A crane; Bem 324] £3

And we were exceedingly fortunate in securing the next *8 Lots*
[lots 322–327 were each "Three framed drawings by Ruskin", and
lots 328–9 each "Two framed drawings by Ruskin"; they are
identified below] at £23.2.0. for the lot, that is, at the rate of
£1.1.0. per drawing, a method of sale evidently peculiar to that
part of the country, since in several instances when a number of
the same items appeared in one lot, the auctioneer sold "at so
much each".

We also purchased:–

Lot 375 – "Coniston Lake" [by Emily Warren, perhaps Bem
             599, Brantwood from the edge of the lake]
             £3.16.0.
    376 – "Feast of Canaan" [by A. Alessandri, after
             Tintoretto, unidentified] £5.5.0.
    378 – T. M. Rooke drawing [Washing-sheds at Chartres;
             Brant 771] £5.10.0.
    379 – J. W. Bunney drawing [N.W. door of St Mark's
             Venice; Brant 707] £6.5.0.
    380 – J. Ruskin drawing ["Mosaic altar piece",
             unidentified] £5.5.0.
    381 – Ditto [Lucca, Guinigi Palace; Bem 1363] £8.15.0.
    400 – Ditto [Lucca, Vineyard Walk; Bem 1369] £13.5.0.
    403 – A. Severn drawing [coastal scene after Turner,
             unidentified] £1.5.0.
    587 – Plaster bust of Ruskin [by Benjamin Creswick]
             £1.0.0.
    635 – A. Severn Coniston Water from Brantwood [?Bem
             507], E. Clifford: Graves of Keats and Severn,
             Rome [Bem 155] £3.10.0.

We also purchased two large bundles of miscellaneous drawings for lectures, which we will go through when they come to
hand next week [Bem 461–5, 467–73, 476, 478–80, 483, 488] £5.

Regarding the third day's sale of books, at the time of writing
we have not yet received a report from our agent who was acting
for us, but as the auctioneer did not anticipate the sale being
ended until 6 or 7 o'clock, and the last post leaves Coniston
nearly four miles away at 5.30, it is probable that we shall not hear
results from our agent until after the holidays, when we will write

The double brougham, built for Ruskin in 1875. In the roof basket is Ruskin's travelling bath

to you further regarding the books and also Lot 787, the single victoria which used to carry Ruskin from London to Coniston.

Regarding this latter item, we understand that Mr Wilkinson (the general factotum of Brantwood, on whose advice the trustees apparently rely implicitly,) has already communicated with you, and we consulted the auctioneers and left it to their discretion to act on our behalf with the full knowledge that the late Mr Arthur Severn had promised this item to you in his life-time, so that possibly the coach may come to you as a gift. In any case we are arranging for the coach to come to London with the other items that we have purchased, as soon as we know the result of the third day's sale.

We purchased a few other items which we shall be pleased to submit to you when they have all been assembled and you can glance through them at your convenience, and when we shall be glad to discuss further the matter of scale of commission, payment of expenses, etc. in relation to this sale.

You will be interested possibly to know that the mahogany bed (Lot 405A) [sold to the buyer of the various study cabinets, and now on loan to Brantwood] in which Ruskin is supposed to have died, sold for £18, and there was much competition for several pieces of finely made furniture, made by Snell & Sons, London, but the large book-case; which you may remember was in the drawing-room (Lots 636–637 and 638) had to be separated, and realised only £16. 10. 0 all told. It probably cost £120 to make.

Reverting to the Ruskin and other drawings, which of course were the principal objects of our attendance at the sale, you may possibly feel that some of the items were high priced, but we acted on the law of averages, and feel that the association direct with Brantwood, will outweigh ordinary considerations as to values, and therefore we purchased items against the numerous private collectors present on the second day, taking the view that you would have done likewise had you been present in person.

… We made the acquaintance whilst up there of some other people who had collected items associated with Ruskin, and if for your Museum you would like such things as portions of the family silver, bearing the crest or the initial R, (tea-spoons, etc. etc.), we could assemble quite a nice little collection for £10 or so, and could get them down on approbation if you so desire, and the items would have an intrinsic value quite apart from their association with the master. Have you in your Museum an example of the celebrated Ruskin coal-shovel, which you remember was specially made by the Coniston black-smith, Tom Bowness, at the village smithy at Yewdale Bridge? We think we could persuade the owner of the *original* shovel to part with same for about half a guinea if you would like it. It is still in use in one of the cottages on the estate.

We also ascertained that quite a considerable number of items have been disposed of privately from Brantwood to various dealers and others who have called as visitors. Amongst these items we have had drawn to our attention, a very interesting set of six family miniatures and silhouettes which we understand *in confidence* were acquired through an agent from Miss Severn. They are as follows:–

Silhouettes.   Ruskin as a boy – signed on the back *J*
Ruskin's grandfather – signed on the back *J*
Ruskin's Mother – by Miers, with the London label.
   This latter man was one of the most celebrated silhouettists.

Miniatures (on ivory)

  Mrs Peter Richardson, Ruskin's Aunt Jessie, of Croydon.
  J.R.S.'s Grandfather, and Mrs Catherine ?
  Mrs John Ruskin's Grandmother (?)

These three are pencilled rather indistinctly at the back and we have been unable at the moment to check up the items. Their value, apart from the association, would average *each* £6–£7 we understand, but we can offer the set of six (which the owner will not separate), for the sum of £24 nett. We notice that one of the "Aunts" is illustrated in the Library Edition, volume 35, page 62.

  Awaiting your decision regarding the silhouettes, silver, etc. and thanking you to acknowledge receipt of the cup we trust will reach you in safety.

  Yours faithfully,
  B. F. Stevens & Brown, Ltd.,
  Ralph Brown

The 22 framed drawings by Ruskin which made up lots 322–329 were identified in a later letter to Whitehouse as:

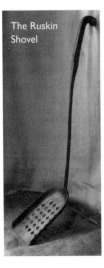
The Ruskin Shovel

Stones of Venice –

  Inlaid marbles (perhaps Brant 1068; *Stones* I, pl. 1)
  Spandril decoration (Brant 1041; *Stones* I, pl. XIV)
  Drawing for plate 74 (unidentified)
  Brick archivolt (Brant 1027)
  Studies of mosaics (Brant 1059; *Stones* II, pl. IV)
  Gothic canopies (Brant 923; *Stones* II, pl. XII)
  Romanesque capitals (unidentified)
  Bases of pillars (Brant 1037; *Stones* I, pl. XII)
  Mouldings (Brant 1051; *Examples*, pl. 14)
  Arch masonry (Brant 862; *Stones* I, pl. IV)
  Peacocks and crosses (Brant 1028; *Stones* II, pl. XI)
  Severe and florid gothic (unidentified)
  Edge decoration (Brant 1042; *Stones* I, pl. IX)
  Renaissance and Romanesque masonry (Brant 978;
    Stones I, pl. XIII)
Courmayeur, from the Col de la Seigne, 1849 (Brant 903)
Florence, Ponte Vecchio, 1872, pencil (possibly Bem 1258)
Verona, Scala monument, 2 sketches in one mount (Brant 1074)

Carvings of crosses and peacocks, studies
made by Ruskin in Venice

Ruskin's study of the mosaics in St Mark's
of the Doge, the Clergy and the People

Ruskin's drawing of the tower and cloister of S. Francesco, Pisa, formerly called the Guinigi Palace

Egyptian sarcophagus in British Museum (we have a number of
    Egyptian subjects; this is unidentified)
Shield at Lucca (Brant 939)
Amiens, sculptured heads (Brant 857 or 858)
Alpine ravine (unidentified)
Chamouni, Glacier de Bois (there are several drawings of this
    subject in the collection)

These and the following drawings provided Whitehouse with impor-
tant additions to his collection: the fine Vineyard Walk at Lucca,
1874 (Bem 1369), recently identified by Paul Tucker as a drawing
of the campanile of a small Romanesque church in the hamlet of
Pozzuolo, just south-west of Lucca; the drawing of the "Mosaic
Altar piece", which is probably Ruskin's study of the mosaics in
St Mark's depicting The Doge, The Clergy and the People, 1876
(Brant 1060); and the drawing which has always been called "The
Tower of the Guinigi Palace, Lucca", 1845, but which has recently
been identified by Paul Tucker as the cloister and tower of San
Francesco, Pisa (Bem 1363).

The large bundles of drawings for lectures represent work by Ruskin and his various secretaries and assistants. They vary in size and are visual aids for many of Ruskin's lectures. Others in the same category which were not in the sale were ultimately given to the collection by Mr Peter Evans.

The purchase of so many drawings made as illustrations for *Stones of Venice* was a valuable addition to the already large group of related material in the collection.

The plaster bust (lot 587) is by Benjamin Creswick. It was modelled at Brantwood in 1877, and I refer to it later.

Brown's conversation with Mr Wilkinson and the auctioneer about Ruskin's coach (lot 787) prompted Violet Severn to write to Whitehouse on 29 July: "I heard … that my Father said he would give you the carriage … so if you care to have it, and my Father told you he would give it to your Museum … I will see that his wishes are carried out." Violet said that it was not included in the catalogue; in fact, she probably knew more about it than the cataloguer, who *had* included it as lot 787, describing it as a "Single Victoria, lamps and cushions complete", and thus it was not noticed by Violet. It is, in fact, a double brougham, and was specially built to Ruskin's specifications in 1875 by the Camberwell coachbuilder Tucker for Ruskin's 1876 posting tour from London via Sheffield to Coniston. Brown was in the process of making arrangements to have the coach sent to Bembridge by goods train when Whitehouse told him to leave it at Brantwood. Ruskin's boat, the *Jumping Jenny*, and his Bath chair, which are also in the collection, may also have been given by Violet Severn to Whitehouse at this time – or they may merely have been left over from the sale! Whitehouse took up the offer of the "Ruskin shovel" and it is now at Brantwood (Bem R 32). He also eventually received a collection of Brantwood silver, which is referred to above.

The family miniatures, which were being offered to Whitehouse through Brown, were in the possession of the Grasmere dealer T. H. Telford. Although they were offered, Telford was loath to part with them for inspection, because he also hoped that they might be bought by a visitor to Grasmere Sports, which were about to take place. He was also looking for a possible American sale. The negotiations continued for some time, Whitehouse having offered substantially less then Telford's asking price, until they finally broke down – presumably because they were bought by the Ruskin scholar from New York, Helen Gill Viljoen. But, curiously, Telford never forgave Whitehouse for not buying them – and he was still aggrieved when I first visited his shop in about 1958.

Appendix – Ruskin's Diaries

C&W no.	R's no.	Bem no.	Soth lot no.	Date	R's date on back	Transc. no.	Non-Bem owner	Notes & Ruskin's name for volume
i				1830			Morgan	
ii		1	1	1835				
iii		3	3	1840,1844		3		
iv	2	2	2			2		
v	4	4	4			4		
vi	5	5A	5			}5A		
vii	5B	5B	6			}5B		
viii	6	5C	7			5		Numbered 5C on slip cover; 5 on binding
ix	7	6	8			6		Sotheby's cat. says 181pp ms ends at p.153 – but first 22pp cut out. Therefore 153–22=131 – Sotheby's misprinted to 181!
x	M	10	9	1849–50		7A		M Venice notebook
xi	M2			1850		7B	Yale	M2 Venice notebook
xii	12	8	11	1851–2		8		
xiii	15	9	12			9		Jib
xiv	10	10A	10			10A		Turner/Missals/Index/Var.
xv		11	13		1856–62			Savoy Flora
xvi }		12	14		1861, 62, 63}	12		Rock Book B 'Geol. Switz'
xvii }					}	12A		NB. 2 vols of transcripts
xviii								
xix		14	15	1866–7		14		Wedderburn's 'Small Book A'
xx		15	16	1867–70		15		Abbeville
xxi		16	17		1869–74			Palermo
		17	18					Egypt/Arabia/Hera/Persia
xxii		18	Soth1931 lot 32		1871–3			Begins with JJR's list of tours
xxiii		19	19		1874–5 1875			St Martins
xxiv		20	20		1876			Broadlands
xxv		21	22		1876–7 1878			Plato/Venice
xxvi		22	21		1864			Myths. Botany D. Contains transcript of his first *Horae*
xxvii				1876–81 1883			Morgan	'Brantwood Diary'
xxviii		23	23	1882–83	1882–3			
xxix		24	24	1884				
xxx								
xxxi		25	25	1885–7				
xxxii		7	26	c1888				Late 1880s? *Praeterita* Notes? "26" marked inside
xxxiii		26	27	1888				

CHAPTER VI

AFTERMATH OF THE SALES

The next few months saw Whitehouse being offered many of the items which had been bought by various dealers at the sales, and he continued to be a willing buyer. For example, in July the bookseller Henry Danielson sold him a copy of Shelley's *Essays, Letters from Abroad*, 1845, inscribed by Joseph Severn to Ruskin.

On 21 August Brown reported that he had heard from the book dealer with whom he had an arrangement regarding the books from the third day of Brantwood's sale. The Carlisle dealer had "managed to sort out from the lorry-load which he had purchased at the sale" the items which Whitehouse and Brown had marked on the viewing day. The 33 items now on offer to Brown for £20 included many presentation copies or books extensively annotated by Ruskin. Here, for example, was John James Ruskin's *Book of Common Prayer*, 1829, Moxon's edition of Chaucer, 1843, the *History of Latin Christianity*, 1854–5, 6 vols, Mrs Jameson's *Sacred and Legendary Art*, 1837, 2 vols, John James Ruskin's copy of Loudon's *Architectural Magazine* containing Ruskin's "Poetry of Architecture" articles, Sismondi's *Histoire des Républiques Italiennes*, 1838, 3 vols, and a number of the classics, including Cary's Dante, 1870. Whitehouse agreed to take them all.

One offer that Whitehouse did not take up was for a cast of the bronze figure of Ruskin sculpted by the American Gutzon Borglum, who is perhaps better known for his mountain carvings of presidents in the Black Hills of Dakota. The statue, which is about 14 inches high, shows Ruskin seated in his study armchair; when casts appear on the market now, they are offered for substantially more than Whitehouse would have had to pay!

The portraits of John James Ruskin and his wife Margaret, by George Watson and James Northcote respectively, which were in the picture sale of May 1931 came up at Sotheby's again in November of that year. There is no record of Whitehouse's bids, but they brought respectively £22 and £38. They were bought either at this sale or subsequently by Mrs Atthill, who was a descendant of Ruskin's cousin Mary Richardson. Mrs Atthill eventually placed the pictures permanently in the collection at Brantwood.

In a sale at Sotheby's on 14 June 1932 Brown bought various lots for Whitehouse. Lot 181 comprised nine letters from Ruskin to Thomas Carlyle and these were secured for £16 (Bem B XIV). Whitehouse had telephoned his instructions to Brown that morning and, in confirming the bid in writing, he also asked Brown to find out who had bought lot 117. This lot was a group of printer's proofs and Whitehouse wrote: "I should like to purchase this lot if it is available at a moderate increase on what was paid for it, but I do not want it at a fanciful price."

Brown had to admit that he had bought it himself for £4 10s. "on behalf of an American correspondent, and we are writing to inquire if he would be disposed to sell". This drew the aggrieved response: "I hope you will forgive my saying that in view of our friendly relationships, and the large amount of business I have been able to place in your hands, that you did not advise me of any items such as Lot 117, and enquire what my wishes are with regard to it." Replying, Brown assured Whitehouse that "this omission shall not occur again". In fact, it appears from the correspondence that the lot was not, after all, printer's proofs, but a group of drawings, "two of the drawings being merely scraps of note-paper with pencil lines on them and a watercolour drawing of a wild hyacinth of no great importance and artistically of no interest, except for the super-scription by Carlyle 'given to me by Ruskin'".

Meanwhile, in three different sales at Hodgson's in July White-house bought lots containing eight parcels of about 130 books, including 30 by Ruskin, a set of *Fors Clavigera* bound in full yellow grained calf by de Coverley, and a large paper edition of *Præterita* in the original parts.

Walker's Gallery of Bond Street often included Ruskin drawings in its stock and in its periodical exhibitions. Often these were offered to Whitehouse through Stevens & Brown. On 19 July a collection of five interesting watercolours or drawings were sent on approval by this route. The group included the ?1832 drawing of Dover Castle from the west (Bem 1234), which Ruskin described as "My first attempt at 'Composition from Nature', Mr Gastineau's sky with my own 'Dover Castle' the latter done out of my head! All dark side and no shadow. This was literally my first attempt at picture-making, at twelve years old. Infinitely stupid, but showing steady power and will to work." Another drawing in the group is described as "Lucca 1882, pencil". There are three 1882 Lucca drawings in the collection; the drawing of the cathedral of San Martino (Brant 938) is in pencil with a touch of watercolour; the sketch of the Lucca hills across Serchio (Bem 1364) is entirely in pencil but is quite slight. The most probable candidate is Brant 941, which is a street scene with the side of the Guinigi Palace, in pencil, merely inscribed "Lucca J.R. 1882".

Another drawing in this lot was a pen and ink study of Turner's Okehampton Castle (Brant 1016). The "Venetian Palace, watercolour, £68.5.0." must have been a fine drawing, if one is to judge by the price. The fifth drawing in the group was the important ?1846 watercolour of the mosaics in the façade of the church of San Miniato al Monte, Florence (Brant 913).

The total price for the five drawings was £122 17s.; Whitehouse wrote to Brown: "The price which Walker's suggest appears to me

Mosaics on the façade of S. Miniato, Florence, a large watercolour
probably made by Ruskin in 1846

quite grotesque, and I think it is hardly worthwhile attempting negotiations on such a basis, for none of the pictures are specially good examples of Ruskin's Work." Whitehouse's itemised offer totalled £41 1s.; incredibly, except for the Venetian palace drawing, the offer was accepted, so he bought the four drawings for £26 1s.

At about this time Whitehouse must have visited Brown's office, for he wrote: "Regarding the drawings by Ruskin which you saw here, as you know we feel that these, as examples of Ruskin's art, are far superior to anything that Walker's have ..." The drawings which Whitehouse had seen in London were Ruskin's 1840–41 study of the Trevi Fountain in Rome (Bem 1467), an 1841 drawing of Pompeii (either Brant 973 or 974), and the fine large study of Abbeville showing the church of St Wulfran from the river, 1868 (Bem 1100). Brown pointed out that this last drawing was coveted by the British Museum and had been the highest-priced drawing, at £210, in the 1907 Ruskin exhibition at The Fine Art Society – and he was offering to let Whitehouse have it for £50; the Trevi Fountain was offered for £30 – or £75 for the two. Negotiations dragged on and eventually they were sent to Bembridge – at £45 and £40 – £85 for the pair!

Soon afterwards, the Scottish dealer who had bought many of the books at the Brantwood sale sent a further list of volumes – 24 titles in 46 volumes – together with two wash drawings by Arthur Severn of the Ruskin houses at Herne Hill and Denmark Hill (Brant 795 and 794) made for Collingwood's *Life and Work of John Ruskin*, 1893 – £35 for the lot. The offer was accepted, bringing to Bembridge such volumes as Stanley's *Memorials of Westminster Abbey*, 1869, Lord Lindsay's *History of Christian Art*, 1847, 3 vols, a couple of volumes of Scott, *Marmion* and *Lady of the Lake*, Alexander Adam's *Summary of Geography and History*, 1794, inscribed "Ex libris Joannis Stewart 1801 To J. J. Ruskin Esq.", John James's copy of Adam's *Roman Antiquities*, 1819, a five-volume edition of *Le Roman de la Rose*, with many notes and markings, a six-volume set of Xenophon, 1817–1821, and Lenormant and De Witte's *Elite des Monuments Ceramographiques*, 1844, in four volumes, with many annotations and with the fore-edges of the text pages trimmed to allow the plates to protrude, for ease of use!

This was another important addition to the ever-growing collection of works from Ruskin's library.

CHAPTER VII

BRANTWOOD

What happened at Brantwood immediately after the sale of the remaining contents is not very clear. There must have been some furniture remaining in the house. For example, the long dining-table does not appear in the sale catalogues, and I can find no reference to it in correspondence. It is known to have been there in 1937, and it seems probable that it never left the house. Perhaps Whitehouse acquired it directly from Violet Severn.

Violet Severn, in fact, probably continued to live at Brantwood for some time. She was certainly still living at Brantwood *during* the sale, when she wrote from there about the carriage. She did not buy No. 1 Lake Villas, a substantial house on the then undeveloped Lake Road in Coniston, until 28 September 1932, so unless she rented the property before she bought it, she presumably remained at Brantwood, with the furniture that she had retained for her own use.

In fact, just before Violet bought No. 1 Lake Villas, and presumably left Brantwood, there was an interesting and little-known exhibition there. I have never seen a reference to it or publicity relating to it; all I am aware of is the four-page catalogue in its yellow ochre covers. The catalogue, which cost 6d. and gave admission to the exhibition, was printed by Milner's of Barrow, but gives no indication of who arranged the exhibition. The exhibition, which was held from 7 to 11 and 14 to 18 September [1932], was of "Watercolours by the late Arthur Severn, R.I., and other artists".

The catalogue lists 133 pictures and "also a numerous amount of unframed water-colour drawings by the late Arthur Severn, R.O.I., R.I.". As well as Severn's watercolours (which included his water-colour of The Devil's Motor Car, an illustration for Marie Corelli's book of the same title), there are examples of the work of Ruskin (three drawings), Mrs Collingwood, C. Richardson, C. Blackwood, F. M. Lytte, F. S. Shills, H. R. Newman and Reginald Barratt. There were also a few oils – Arthur Severn's portrait of W. G. Collingwood and a group of copies of Old Masters by Joseph Severn.

A comparison of the picture titles in this catalogue with the list of watercolours by Arthur Severn which Miss Horne withdrew from the Warwick Square sale shows that they are substantially the same. There are, in fact, a few more in the exhibition than were withdrawn from the sale, and they probably represent the final sweepings of Warwick Square and Brantwood. There is no indication in the catalogue of either prices or the organiser's identity. However, it is probably safe to assume that the exhibition was the work of Miss Horne.

After the picture sale and Violet Severn's almost immediate removal into Coniston, Brantwood was now really deserted (save for the Wilkinsons living in the lodge) and quieter than it had ever been throughout the 135 years of its life.

Originally built as a cottage of eight rooms, Brantwood in the 1790s stood on some three acres of steep, rocky and wooded land. But both house and grounds grew. An early owner, Ann Copley, extended the house by the addition of another room at the front, and some rooms at the rear in the kitchen area. She also added the six-acre Jackson Low Wood to the estate in 1833. This plot then provided the site for the stable block, kitchen gardens and grounds behind them.

W. J. Linton, republican, printer and wood engraver, lived at Brantwood from 1852 until 1871 (although he had emigrated to

Albert Goodwin's watercolour of part of the view from Brantwood

Brantwood today is very much larger than the cottage Ruskin bought in 1871. The Severns' additions may be seen on the extreme left. To the right is the Lodge, built in 1872–3 by Ruskin for his valet, and farther right are the stables and coach house. The field in the foreground is Ruskin's original "Naboth's Vineyard – my neighbour's field to the water's edge"

America before he sold the house). His contribution to Brantwood's development was to add the bow window to the study and to erect the building on the back drive to house his printing press. When the fells were enclosed in 1862, the sheep which he grazed entitled him to an apportionment of six acres, which brought the total size of the estate up to about sixteen acres.

This was what Ruskin bought, sight unseen, for £1,500 in 1871. He knew the view; he thought it one of the finest in Europe. It reminded him of Switzerland and he had, in fact, drawn it from the Brantwood shore in 1837 as an illustration for his "Poetry of Architecture" papers in Loudon's *Architectural Magazine*.

During Ruskin's time the house grew, largely to accommodate the ever-growing needs of the Severn family, who were his permanent guests, to a substantial thirty rooms. At first he rented the field across the road from Brantwood and eventually he was able to buy it. Several purchases of surrounding land and property – in Joan Severn's name – in the 1890s increased the size of the estate to about 486 acres and added Lawson Park Farm on the fells above Brantwood, Black Beck Cottage on the road near the northern extremity of the estate, and Low Bank Ground Farm and the large house then called Coniston Bank (now Thurston) on the lake side of the road to the north of Brantwood.

After Ruskin's time, the Severns extended the house still further by increasing the size of the drawing-room (and thus providing Mrs Severn's bedroom above with a balcony) and adding the heptangular block to the north-west corner of the house to provide the boudoir off the drawing-room and a dressing-room above for Arthur Severn.

This was the Brantwood which was offered for sale after the dispersal of the contents by Knight Frank & Rutley, the London estate agents. Coniston Bank had already been sold earlier. For the sale, the remaining estate was split into eight lots and was offered for sale by auction on 20 July 1932, either as a whole or in lots, "unless previously disposed of privately" – but it attracted no bids. We know that Whitehouse had hoped to buy the house and had actually been involved in protracted negotiations with Arthur Severn to do this in the 1920s. The fact that he did not buy it at the sale was an indication that he had made a careful assessment of the situation and had astutely decided that he could do better by waiting.

Whitehouse had a copy of the prospectus for the sale and perhaps had held discussions with the agents in advance about the probable selling price. There would not have been a great demand in 1932 for a rambling semi-derelict house, albeit with literary and artistic associations, together with a small hill farm and 500 acres of fells and rocks, with little grazing even for sheep. At the foot of the prospectus Whitehouse wrote "£6500" – but did not indicate whether this was the likely price for the whole estate or for selected lots.

Since he had decided to play a waiting game, intervention by Ralph Brown must have come as an unwelcome surprise. Brown wrote three days after the abortive auction to say that, after the contents sale, he had asked at the office if the house had been sold and had just received the following letter from Knight Frank & Rutley dated 21 July:

> We write to inform you that this property was not sold at the auction yesterday afternoon, and we are now in a position to deal with it privately. If Mr Brown is interested as a possible buyer, we shall be happy to quote a price upon hearing from you.

Whitehouse acknowledged Brown's letter on the same day, with the injunction: "I should be grateful if you would not communicate further with Knight Frank & Rutley as we have already done so, and the matter is now going forward."

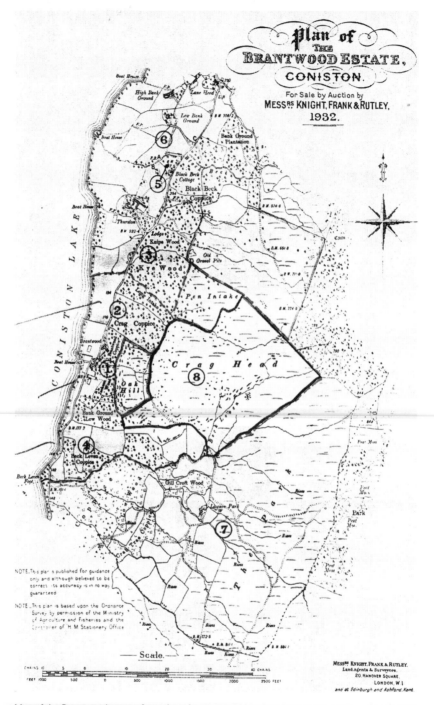

Map of the Brantwood estate, from the sale prospectus

Ultimately the matter *did* go forward; but undoubtedly a lot of negotiating took place first. Whitehouse bought lots 1, 2, 4 and 8, the house and its outbuildings, and the 250 acres of ground immediately surrounding them. The conveyance was signed on 13 December 1932 – and Whitehouse had succeeded in beating the price down to £1,750.

Having bought Brantwood with the intention of opening it to the public as a national memorial to Ruskin, he had to set about fitting it out with exhibits for the public to see and with furniture for himself and others who were to stay there.

Ralph Brown bought a seventeenth-century oak dresser for him in March 1933 which was eventually sent to Brantwood and suggested that he introduce Whitehouse to the firm of S. W. Wolsey of Buckingham Gate who had a very large stock of old oak – but nothing appears to have come of that idea. Later in the year Stevens & Brown found for Whitehouse a badly water-stained set of the *Library Edition*; Whitehouse extracted almost all the plates and had them framed to help decorate the walls.

Finally, Brantwood was ready for the opening. Brown had an invitation but wasn't sure whether a prior engagement would keep him away. It didn't and, on his return to London, he wrote: "It gave the writer very much pleasure to be present at Brantwood last Saturday and he wishes to record his congratulations to you on the culmination of your untiring efforts towards the preservation of the memory of John Ruskin."

The formal opening ceremony for Brantwood was held at 3 p.m. on Saturday 21 April 1934. Some fifty guests attended by invitation and others wrote expressing their delight in, and support for, what Whitehouse was doing. He took the chair and no doubt revelled in the event – enjoying this as he always did such occasions.

The opening attracted both national and local press coverage. The *Manchester Guardian* reported:

Brantwood, the house beside Coniston Water, where Ruskin spent the last thirty years of his life, was opened today as a national memorial to him … The occasion was in the nature of a personal triumph for Mr J. Howard Whitehouse, President of the Ruskin Society, whose hard work and generosity have been largely responsible for saving the estate …

One of the principal guests was Whitehouse's old parliamentary friend Isaac Foot, M.P., who, in the words of *The Times*:

> spoke of the service rendered to the country by John Ruskin and paid a tribute to Mr Whitehouse, who, he said, was one of those who thought it his life's work to see that the name of Ruskin was held in proper reverence ... He spoke of the quickening of the social conscience which was largely attributable to the reading of Ruskin. It was most fitting that the place where Ruskin spent the happiest part of his life should be maintained for ever as a public property.

The Mayor of Lancaster, Councillor H. Warbrick, who was also present, proposed a vote of thanks and "voiced appreciation of so excellent a national memorial".

At the end of the proceedings tea was served by the resident host and hostess, Mr and Mrs Kenneth Romney-Townrow. The leaflet that Whitehouse issued to coincide with the opening, *Brantwood, The home of John Ruskin, A brief statement of its foundation as a national memorial to Ruskin*, explained that, in addition to being open to the public, "a part of Brantwood will be used as a Guest House, and applications to stay there, for long or short periods, may be made to the resident host and hostess, or to the honorary secretary to the Ruskin Society, Mr Niel Rocke, at Bembridge School, Isle of Wight."

The Ruskin Society had been established by Whitehouse at a meeting held at the Royal Society of Arts at the beginning of 1932. Over the years the society was to hold regular luncheons or dinners to celebrate Ruskin's birthday and had committed itself to the publication of an annual volume which was usually a collection of the speeches made at these events. In 1935 the sister Friends of Brantwood was founded, and in 1945 or 1946 the two were amalgamated. They were essentially Whitehousian societies; with his increasing age, they declined, eventually disappearing after his death.

In 1937, in *Ruskin and Brantwood*, Whitehouse wrote:

> The house and grounds were offered for sale by auction in London, but without attracting any bidders. The house threatened speedily to become a ruin. Of all the opportunities which have been mine, I look back upon none with more satisfaction and pleasure than being able to acquire the home of John Ruskin and to secure it for the nation.

CHAPTER VIII

1932–1940

Throughout his life Whitehouse maintained an interest in international politics and was always fascinated by processes of government. He also had the knack of being able to brush away bureaucracy or any other problems surrounding people whom he wished to meet.

Mussolini had come to power in Italy in October 1922 and Whitehouse was determined to meet him. "I went to Italy with this intention," he wrote. It was also Whitehouse's wish that the work of Ruskin should be represented in Italian national collections, so, to this end, he took three fine drawings with him.

After a certain amount of delay an appointment was arranged, partly through the good offices of the British Ambassador, and thus it was that in April 1932 Whitehouse met Mussolini. Writing later, he recorded the event:

I had been warned that he received his visitors in one of the great halls belonging to the nobles who had been deposed, and that Mussolini himself sat at the far end of this great room, and I would not know at first what kind of reception I should receive. These statements did not alarm me. I not only went myself but I took a young friend with me, hoping that I should be able to get him in. At the outside door my credentials were examined, and the guard passed me. Then he noticed my young friend, looking at him he said "Your son?" I replied "No, I am his guardian." And as they had no idea what I meant, there was no further difficulty at this or at other check points.

I was not immediately shown into Mussolini's presence but we were conducted to a small room to await my turn. This was a very interesting place, and the walls were lined with cases full of beautiful things stolen by Mussolini. It was interesting to me to see the people who were also waiting for an audience. Three of Mussolini's ministers arrived, very beautifully dressed; and altogether they stepped forward to examine one of the pictures, but they were only using the glass as a mirror. They were obviously in great fear of Mussolini. They were followed by one who was an important officer in the army, for he was in magnificent uniform, and a humble soldier carried his accoutrements in front of him.

Finally I was myself summoned to Mussolini. He received me quite politely. I had been warned that if I said anything with which he disagreed his eyes would bulge from his head. I was therefore prepared at this point, and thought myself I would practice the same, but I failed, and did not pursue the method. My talk with Mussolini concerned the war which was then raging in Abyssinia. Also he discussed the possibility of a treaty between Italy, Spain and the United States. He enquired about problems in England, asking how we were treating the Indian trouble. I said it was not serious and that we should soon give them self-government, at which statement his eyes came out.

We had a discussion on other public questions, and then I felt it was time my visit finished, and as we walked down the hall he said he would arrange for me to see his Minister of Education next morning …

I saw Mussolini on a second occasion when we again discussed the international situation. He was most courteous and I presented to him an original water colour drawing by Ruskin, which he accepted. I do not know what its fate was.

In fact, Whitehouse presented two drawings to Mussolini. Both dated from the Italian tour of 1840–41. One was a Florentine view – the view along the Ponte Vecchio looking towards the Duomo, drawn in November 1840 – the other view was of the Piazza Santa Maria del Pianto, Rome. Both drawings are now in the Museo di Roma in Rome.

Another of Whitehouse's aims in Italy was to become personally acquainted with the Pope [Pope Pius XI]:

I achieved an introduction and it was a very remarkable experience for on the day appointed I had to leave my hotel early in the morning in evening dress. When I arrived at the Vatican I was shown into a room of great length and beauty, where the Pope receives important visitors from other countries. I have rarely seen a more remarkable room, both in architecture and gay with

View of the Ponte Vecchio, Florence, one of the pair of drawings by Ruskin which J. H. W. presented to Mussolini

uniforms. The Master of Ceremonies showed me to a seat in this brilliant assembly, and said he would fetch me when the Pope was ready. Our Minister to the Vatican had kindly arranged to accompany me. When we were summoned to the Pope the Minister told me that he was a Catholic and he would have to observe the ritual in front of the Pope. As I was not a Catholic I would not have to do this, but I told the Minister I would rather do exactly what he did, which he said simplified matters. The door to the Pope's private apartment was opened and as we entered we knelt for the blessing by the Pope. Then we walked to the centre of the room, again knelt, and again we were blessed. We then approached his chair, and knelt once more for a third blessing. I presented to the Pope an original drawing by Ruskin. I told him that Ruskin had taught us most of what we know about Italy. The Pope said he collected watercolours and would have great pleasure in adding this to the Papal collection. I also told the Pope that Ruskin bridged the centuries between Pope Julian some hundreds of years ago, and today. He was puzzled as to my meaning. Then I explained that Pope Julian insisted on Michelangelo painting the ceiling of the Sistine Chapel, which meant he

S. Anna a Capuana, Naples, 1841, the drawing by Ruskin which J. H. W. presented to the Pope

must erect a scaffold. Ruskin centuries later had also erected a scaffold in order to copy the work of Michelangelo. At this the Pope smiled.

Whitehouse presented the Pope with an 1841 drawing of S. Anna a Capuana, Naples, which is still preserved in the Biblioteca Apostolica Vaticana (Vat. Lat. 15244).

Meanwhile, the life of Bembridge School continued. The Italian visit had received national press coverage, with positive attendant publicity for the school; and the quest for new items for the collection went on.

There are various drawings of Brantwood in the collection. One of the nicest is a pen and wash drawing of the house from the edge of the lake, drawn in 1892 by Arthur Severn (Brant 782). It is inscribed on the reverse by Joan Severn, "Brantwood – yes, he's done that carefully. J. R." This was bought from Stevens & Brown in October 1932 and is almost the identical view to another by Severn, drawn in charcoal, wash and Chinese white, and bought from the Manning Gallery in 1968 (Bem 500).

Another dealer who bought at the Brantwood sale was Arnold Varty of Ambleside. Through Brown, he offered Whitehouse a

"Yes, he's done that carefully" – Arthur Severn's view of Brantwood from the edge of the lake

parcel of Ruskin drawings in November 1932 which was at first declined, because they were not considered to be by Ruskin. Also offered was a sketchbook formerly belonging to Susan Beever. She had lived at The Thwaite, Coniston, and had been a friend of Ruskin since he moved to Coniston in 1872. She was very knowledgeable in all matters relating to natural history and Ruskin frequently sought her opinion about plants and birds. A selection of Ruskin's letters to her was edited by Albert Fleming in *Hortus Inclusus*. The sketchbook, which was bought from Varty for 30s. (Bem 81), had been given by Susan Beever to Ruskin – it contains his bookplate. Its 24 pages contain a series of beautifully executed studies of flowers, butterflies and birds.

About the same time a miscellaneous collection of 34 volumes by Ruskin was bought from T. F. Taylor of Boston in Yorkshire, and a bid of £1 secured a lot of three Ruskin drawings at Sotheby's on 30 November – a "street in a continental town; architectural study, and Alligator".

Five drawings of a rather different quality were offered through Brown by an unnamed buyer at the Ruskin sales at £36 15s., and were bought for £25. They were Ruskin's copy, made about 1834, of Samuel Prout's lithograph of the Hôtel de Ville, Louvain (Bem

1450), a study in body colour and pencil of rocks and a torrent (Bem 1465), and a Neapolitan street scene drawn in 1841 in pencil and wash (Bem 1409). There are now several studies of the strange rock formations at Malham in Yorkshire in the collection, but the one included in this group of five drawings is probably now Bem 1381. The final drawing in the group (Brant 1006) is of the bridge at Terni, drawn in April 1841 on the journey from Rome to Florence. Ruskin enjoyed the rugged scenery here for a few days, comparing it in his diary with the hills near Matlock in Derbyshire. This dramatic drawing has more than the usual amount of colour for this period, which Ruskin used to great advantage.

For £3 at Sotheby's on 24 March 1933 Brown bought an eighteenth-century bronze copy of "Hermes resting". This has no Ruskin association, but it was a piece which appealed to Whitehouse and it now stands on a stone plinth on the lawn at the side of the approach to the New House and galleries. The original statue, which dates from the 3rd century BC, was found in 1758 in the ruins of a house near Herculaneum which may have belonged to Julius Caesar's father-in-law. It is now in a museum in Naples; a cast is in

A page from Susan Beever's sketchbook

John Ruskin: Rocks and a torrent

the British Museum. The present reduced copy, for which Brown was told not to exceed a bid of £4, was probably also made in the late-eighteenth century.

Among the things which Stevens & Brown had bought for stock at the Brantwood sale was part of Ruskin's collection of daguerreo-types. The daguerreotype was an early form of photographic process developed in 1839 by Louis-Jacques Mandé Daguerre and Joseph-Nicéphore Niepce. The actual image forms on a silver-coated copper plate which has been sensitised with iodine fumes and exposed to mercury vapour after being in the camera. The plate is then protected from damage by a sheet of glass which is fixed in front of the image. Ruskin seems to have first discovered the new art of daguerreotyping in the spring of 1840 (or possibly even 1842). Later he recorded the occasion in *Præterita*:

> It must have been during my last days at Oxford that Mr Liddell, the present Dean of Christ Church told me of the original experiments of Daguerre. My Parisian friends obtained for me the best examples of his result; and the plates sent to me in Oxford were certainly the first examples of the sun's drawing that were ever seen in Oxford, and, I believe, the first sent to England.

Ruskin does not seem to have taken any further interest in the process until his continental tour of 1845. In Pisa in that year he says in letter 20 of *Fors Clavigera*: "I daguerreotyped the eastern end of [the church of S. Maria della Spina] and copied the daguerreotype that people might not be plagued in looking by the lustre." The daguerreotype is now at Bembridge (Bem Dag 62) and the drawing is in the Guild of St George collection in Sheffield.

During the same tour, when in Venice, Ruskin commissioned a "poor Frenchman" to make twenty daguerreotypes for him of buildings, at a cost of one napoleon each. In his letter of 7 October 1845 he told his father that he had bought:

> some most beautiful, though very small, Dags of the palaces I have been trying to draw; and certainly Dags taken in this vivid sunlight are glorious things ... It is a noble invention – say what they will of it – and any one who has worked and blundered and stammered as I have done for four days, and then sees the thing he has been trying to do so long in vain, done perfectly and faultlessly in half a minute, won't abuse it afterwards.

A note in the second volume of *Modern Painters*, 1846, shows that he had been experimenting unsuccessfully with daguerreotypes of foliage, while the preface to the first edition of *Seven Lamps of Architecture*, 1849, shows that he was making practical use of the process. Two of the plates in that book were engraved from daguerreotypes.

One must infer from Ruskin's references that he occasionally took daguerreotypes himself; but he must also have had his various valets trained in the art. In *Præterita*, for example, Ruskin refers to the tour of 1849 and "George (John Hobbs) indefatigably carrying his little daguerreotype box up everywhere and taking the first image of the Matterhorn, as also of the aiguilles of Chamouni ever drawn by the sun". He also refers to this in *Deucalion*: "the first sun portrait ever taken of the Matterhorn (and as far as I know, of any Swiss mountain whatever)". The photographs were taken from Zermatt, probably on Friday or Saturday 3 or 4 August 1849. After John Hobbs left Ruskin's employ, his successor as valet, Frederick Crawley, was also expected to take daguerreotypes, and there are several signed as his work at Bembridge: "The Aiguilles in Chamony Savoy 1854 F. Crawley" (Bem Dag 73), for example, a view of Mont Blanc, 1854 (Bem Dag 74) and an 1856 view of Fribourg (Bem Dag 81).

Ruskin seems to have made extensive use of the process, both for recording details of architecture and as notes for subsequent drawings. In the preface to *Examples of the Architecture of Venice*, 1851, he says that he had not used daguerreotypes for preparing the mezzotints contained in that book, but "much regret that artists in general do not think it worth their while to perpetuate some of the beautiful effects which the daguerreotypes alone can seize". He extolled the virtues of the process again in *Stones of Venice* III, 1853: "A power of obtaining veracity in the representation of material and tangible things, which, within certain limits and conditions, is unimpeachable, has now been placed in the hands of all men, almost without labour."

Ruskin built up a considerable collection of daguerreotypes, principally of architectural studies taken in Italy. There was a large number of Venetian studies, but there were also interesting groups taken in Rouen, Chartres, Rheims and Basle. Because he found the daguerreotypes so successful and useful, he probably continued to commission or take them after the process had been superseded by photography.

Bem MS 27 is a note-book used by Ruskin which formed part of lot 32 at Sotheby's on 18 May 1931, the lot which also contained the fugitive diary volume for 1871–73. The present volume, titled by Ruskin on the spine "Coins", contains the catalogue of his very substantial collection of Greek and Roman coins. Here too he has listed the miniatures and illuminated letters in the three volumes of his thirteenth-century Beaupré Antiphoner. In this same volume Ruskin also listed 250 of his daguerreotypes and gave them all a catalogue number, indicating also in some cases whether the daguerreotype was L[arge] or S[mall].

The 125 daguerreotypes which Brown offered to Whitehouse for £5 on March 1933 thus represent only part of Ruskin's collection, which in fact must have numbered more than 250. Some of the Bembridge daguerreotypes have their Ruskin catalogue numbers written on them, but there are also many here which are not listed in Ruskin's catalogue. Accompanying the collection is a mahogany box with brass handles which Ruskin had made to contain the daguerreotypes taken in Tuscany in 1846.

Whitehouse was interested in several of the lots in the J. Pritchard Gordon sale at Sotheby's on 10 May 1933, but unfortunately the bids which he left with Brown were too low and he only succeeded in buying three lots – Samuel Prout's Old Street in Lisieux (lot 61, £15; Brant 764), which had been included in Ruskin's Prout and Hunt exhibition at The Fine Art Society in 1879, and Ruskin's fine large Walls of Lucerne (lot 64, £13; Bem 1376). He also paid 8 guineas for the large watercolour of Paestum by Paul Naftel which had been bought by Pritchard under Ruskin's guidance from the 1861 Old Water Colour Society's exhibition (No. 88). Ruskin often mentioned Naftel's work favourably in *Academy Notes*, but he does not appear to have written about Paestum (Brant 755).

Two other lots, 62 and 63, were sold to Walker's Gallery for £12 and £25: Ruskin's Square at Cologne, 1842, one of the very last drawings in his early Proutesque style (Bem 1220), given by Ruskin to Miss Pritchard; and the beautiful 1862–3 drawing of the view from the base of the Brezon looking towards Geneva, with the Jura in the distance and the Salève on the left (Bem 1174). Brown had not been allowed to bid enough to secure these two important drawings in the sale, so Whitehouse had to pay Walker the hammer price, *plus* 10 guineas as his profit.

John Pritchard, who had originally established this collection of pictures, was married to the sister of Rev. Osborne Gordon, Ruskin's private tutor at Oxford. Pritchard himself was John James Ruskin's solicitor and executor of his will; he went into Parliament as the member for Bridgnorth. The collection eventually descended to, and was disposed of by, H. Pritchard Gordon, the great nephew of the original collector.

In the same month as the Pritchard Gordon sale, the booksellers Maggs Bros. offered Whitehouse a substantial manuscript, the 124 leaves of *Our Fathers have told us*, Part 1, The Bible Amiens, and notes and general plan for Part 2, which he bought for £21 (Bem MS 46). This manuscript had originally been lot 120 in the books and manuscripts sale at Sotheby's on 24 July 1930, where Maggs appear to have paid £22 for it.

Remembering that they had bought the Samuel Laurence portrait of Ruskin for Whitehouse in 1927, Ralph Brown reported that a portrait of Thomas Carlyle by the same artist was being offered by Robinson & Fisher in their sale on 8 June, and it was knocked down for 8 guineas without meeting the reserve. Brown suggested offering 5 guineas for it and, after some indecision, it was secured for the collection at £7 (Brant 742).

A sale at Christie's on the next day contained a group of Ruskin drawings with an interesting association. They had belonged to a Miss Harrison, who was almost certainly one of the daughters of

Trees near Turin: Ruskin's drawing of 1846

Ruskin's "first editor", W. H. Harrison. Stevens & Brown advised Whitehouse that the two lots should not bring more than £3 or £4 each. However, they must have been allowed some discretion, as they bought both for the collection. Lot 76 comprised the pair of 1845 watercolours of Château Lausanne – at moonrise and sunrise (Bem 1342 and 1343, 10 guineas); there were four drawings in lot 77 – secured for 3½ guineas – the large View on the Coast of Normandy, 1848 (Brant 966), which Ruskin had drawn when he was on his first continental tour with his new wife; the drawing catalogued as "Forest near Milan" is in fact Trees near Turin, 1 May 1846 (Brant 1014); the drawing of Vesuvius in eruption (Brant 1080) is one of at least three which Ruskin made of this subject in 1841 in a style quite unlike that usually employed on the tour; the final drawing in the lot was a small view of the lake of Thun, attributed, improbably, to Turner (Bem 576).

Books were not neglected while buying all these drawings. Included in Hodgson's sale on 27 July 1933 was J. P. Smart's collection of Ruskin material. Smart had been the secretary of the Ruskin Society of London and had collaborated with T. J. Wise in his Ruskin bibliography. Smart had built up a substantial collection of material, including copies of several of Wise's Ruskin publications. Brown bought nine lots for Whitehouse for a total of £12 18s. He let the set of the *Library Edition* go to "a provincial dealer" for £10, but he obtained a mass of material, much of it scarce and ephemeral, for the collection. Lot 181, for example, contained "several large newspaper cuttings books, the papers of the Ruskin Society of London, and very many pamphlets. If necessary we will go to 20s. to secure them." In the event, Brown had to pay £3 15s. for the lot, although the next lot, two portfolios of material, including between 40 and 50 impressions of the Elliot & Fry photograph of Ruskin which forms the frontispiece to the Wise-Smart *Bibliography*, for which Brown expected to pay £2, fell to him for £1 9s.

The letters from Ruskin to his mother which had been included in the Warwick Square sale came on the market again in 1933. The 395 letters, written between 1866 and 1871, had originally been catalogued in 1931 as seven lots. However, they had been put together and sold as one lot for £90. We do not know what Whitehouse's bid had been, because he had telephoned his instructions to Brown at the last moment, finding it impossible to attend the sale in person. The letters had been bought by the London dealer Michelmore, who had them mounted and bound in full blue morocco gilt by Rivière. It seems that he was asking about £500 for the now sumptuously clothed collection but, unable to find a buyer, he offered them at Sotheby's on 31 July 1933.

Whitehouse very much wanted this important group of letters, to complement the mass of family letters which he already owned. On 27 July Brown reported that, in his opinion, the volume would bring £150–180, an estimate confirmed by Sotheby's. Whitehouse replied that, although he very much hoped that Brown would buy the letters for him, he "cannot go beyond a moderate price" and authorised a maximum bid of £205, "though if an extra pound or two would get them, I am willing to give you a little discretion".

In the event, despite bidding against Maggs up to £215, the letters did not reach the reserve, which it later transpired was £275. On the day after the sale, Brown, as the underbidder, received a letter from Michelmore offering him the volume for £215, but later in the morning Michelmore telephoned to withdraw the offer, because they had heard that Sotheby's had received an offer of £250. It subsequently transpired that the new offer had been made by the

American dealers Henry Stevens Son & Stiles, bidding on behalf of an American collector. Protracted and increasingly involved negotiations continued throughout August and because Whitehouse went to Brantwood during their course, Brown was duplicating his letters to both Bembridge and Coniston to ensure that Whitehouse was kept up to date with the proceedings.

Michelmore delayed making a decision to accept Sotheby's offer, and meanwhile Brown offered £240 (taking the commission into account, about the same as Michelmore would net if he accepted the £250 offer with Sotheby's). However, this amount must have been insufficient, because on 2 August Brown sent the volume of letters to Bembridge for Whitehouse's examination, urging him either to let Sotheby's know immediately that he would not buy them or to make an offer in excess of £250 – "their customer is exceedingly impatient and is pressing for an answer".

Whitehouse offered £251, but Sotheby's agent, Mr de Graz, said that he could not recognise this increase in his capacity as an auctioneer, and suggested £260 would be appropriate. Brown suggested that £255 would be more in keeping and this offer was made to Sotheby's, who replied that, since Whitehouse would not pay £260, they could not accept his offer and "the letters have been disposed of to another buyer whose offer was substantially in excess of what you kindly conveyed to us".

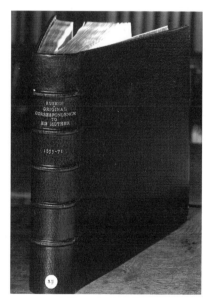

The volume containing Ruskin's letters to his mother, 1853–71

But they hadn't taken into consideration Whitehouse's determination to keep the letters which by now were in his hands. Sotheby's request that the letters be returned to them incensed Whitehouse, who telegraphed Brown on 10 August: "Letters given to Ruskin Trust definitely offered me for any sum over £250 cannot return please consult solicitor."

Meetings took place between Sotheby's and the solicitors, and it emerged that, if Whitehouse offered £275, an endeavour would be made to persuade the rival buyer to consent to the cancellation of the contract. Brown urged Whitehouse to return the letters immediately, assuring him that all were agreed he had no legal claim. However, nothing daunted, Whitehouse replied: "I have decided to contest the matter"; he thought he had been "so strangely treated" that he would let his solicitor deal with the affair. Then he made his final offer: "Give the owner the sum he has now been offered."

Brown met with Michelmore, offered £275, and asked them to persuade Sotheby's to cancel the contract with their other client, Henry Stevens Son & Stiles. Meanwhile Whitehouse wrote again: "I have decided to contest this matter in the courts if your offer is not accepted, for I feel that I have been treated with very great injustice."

No doubt to his great relief, Brown was able to telegraph to Whitehouse on 21 August that he was "making amicable settlement", and on the following day he reported on the meeting

Some of Ruskin's chessmen

between himself, Mr Solomon of Michelmore's, and Mr Tree of Henry Stevens Son & Stiles. Tree agreed to cancel the contract with Sotheby's if Brown paid him the difference between the £255 offered by Whitehouse and the £275 he was to have paid Sotheby's on behalf of his American client; provided that Michelmore's accepted the £255, they were to settle Sotheby's commission. Meanwhile Whitehouse was to pay the balance of £20 to Brown to enable him to pay Tree! All very involved – but "I will accept this. I think you have been badly treated both by Sotheby's and Michelmore's and am sorry that I have to pay the further £20. But I will do so in order to save any further trouble either to yourselves or to me."

So, with this letter of 23 August, the matter ended, with Whitehouse in possession of the letters (Bem B VI) which he had held since 2 August. No doubt he quietly wished that he had offered enough to buy them two years earlier at the Warwick Square sale.

In September 1933 Stevens & Brown sent Whitehouse an eight-page list of drawings by Ruskin and others, and items of Ruskin association, which they had bought for their own stock at Brantwood. The items were priced individually and totalled £545 14s. 6d.

Among the Ruskiniana were such things as Ruskin's chess set, six brass finger-bowls, a collection of wine glasses, the boxes of daguerreotypes about which Whitehouse had still not made a decision, a silver spoon-warmer, two silver studs, Ruskin's father's silver wine-strainer, Ruskin's bronze candlesticks and bronze ink pot, and the mahogany marble and glass shell cabinet from the drawing-room, with the collection of shells.

The list of drawings included several which had been offered before and over which decisions had not been reached – Abbeville's St Wulfran from the river, 1868 (Bem 1100), and the Trevi Fountain, Rome, 1840 (Bem 1467). Here also were the Glacier des Bois, c. 1840, reproduced in *Friendship's Offering* for 1843 (Brant 893), Lake Brienz from the Giessbach Hotel, 1866 (Bem 1176), The Light in the West – Beauvais Cathedral (Bem 1146), and the large wash drawing of a bird's talon (Bem 1154). Pencil drawings included an 1841 study of Pompeii (Brant 973 or 974), the 1835 study of the Castelbarco Tomb at Verona (Bem 1647) and a study of the Glacier des Bois drawn for *Modern Painters*, ?1856 (Bem 1205).

Drawings by other artists which had come from Brantwood included T. M. Rooke's Wedding at Chartres, 1885 (Bem 430).

Ruskin's study candlesticks, his bronze inkwell, a silver spoon-warmer and his father's silver wine-strainer

Ruskin had been very enthusiastic about the series of drawings that Rooke had made for him that year at Chartres, and of this drawing and another he wrote: "Of all the lovely thoughts and things I've ever seen painted, these two last beat." In this watercolour he particularly liked the cat sitting on the window-sill, watching the darting swallow. Bunney was represented by a watercolour "From the north door of the Duomo of Florence" (Brant 708), and an architectural study of a cathedral (Brant 706) and a river scene by John Linnell (Brant 743). Portraits included Arthur Severn's imaginative portrait of Ruskin as a small boy sketching in a landscape (Bem 526) and the fine portrait of John James Ruskin by George Richmond which had been made in 1848 as a wedding present for John (Bem 420).

Portraits by George Richmond are unmistakable, and a comparison of this portrait with later photographs of the hard-headed Scottish businessman clearly show that Richmond had "improved" his subject! Travelling in the same coach together to John James Ruskin's funeral in 1864 were George Richmond, Sir John Simon and Arthur Severn. The conversation turned to art and portraiture and the way in which artists improved their subjects. Simon said firmly, that "A portrait should represent the truth, and nothing but the truth." "Ah," said Richmond, "but the truth lovingly told."

Castelbarco Tomb, Verona, 1835, by Ruskin

Whitehouse was very tempted by Brown's list, and at first agreed to take "some" of the association items, including the chessmen. Then in October he told Brown to send the shell cabinet to Brantwood.

Later in October the ink well was sent, and in November the daguerreotypes, the silver and glass, and three small cabinets of framed Turner engravings which had not appeared on the original list. Finally, in January 1934, the remaining association items and most of the pictures (some had already come to Bembridge) were sent to Brantwood. Whitehouse had succeeded in obtaining the whole collection, originally offered at a total of £545 14s. 6d., for the reduced figure of £300.

Inevitably there are retrospective regrets – but Whitehouse could not have bought *all* that he was offered. One of these regrets must be the refusal to buy the Ruskin–Swan correspondence which is now in the collection of the Philip H. & A. S. W. Rosenbach Foundation in Philadelphia. Henry Swan was one of Ruskin's pupils in the drawing class at the Working Men's College, and when Ruskin established the Guild of St George Museum at Walkley in Sheffield in 1875, he put Swan and his wife in charge. Swan was the sort of interesting and eccentric character that Ruskin seemed to attract. A vegetarian, Quaker and spiritualist, he was among the first to introduce the bicycle into this country; he tried and failed to promote boomerang-throwing as an athletic exercise. Before he settled in

"The truth lovingly told" – George Richmond's portrait of John James Ruskin, 1848

Sheffield, Swan had worked as an engraver on the plates for Pitman's shorthand publications. Later he had set up a photographic business in Regent Street and perfected a type of photographic miniature portrait. He was also an accomplished illuminator; when in London, he copied manuscripts in the British Museum for Ruskin.

During their friendship, up to the time of Swan's death in 1889, some 350 letters were written by Ruskin to Swan and his wife Emily. This correspondence contains much valuable information about the growth and development of the guild collection. By 1916 this group of letters was in New York, in the hands of the prominent dealer Gabriel Wells. He had had the letters and a transcript of each bound by Sangorsky and Sutcliffe in ten volumes at a cost of nearly £100. He had placed a value of about £700 on the collection but, as a result of the depression, was looking for a buyer for the letters. Ralph Brown was in America in November 1933 and Wells had asked him if he could "interest my customer in them at some considerably less sum". Brown brought away with him the first volume, containing about 30 letters, and tried to interest Whitehouse in the collection for about £350. The volume was examined and duly returned to Stevens & Brown within a few days but, employing his usual delaying tactics, Whitehouse did not commit himself to their purchase. By January 1934 Brown was asking Whitehouse if he wanted to buy the manuscript of *Lectures on Art*, which Wells was also selling, for £105. In March Brown offered Whitehouse another option on the letters, saying that he was about to return the volume to America; however, he wrote again in July for a final answer. In August and September, when Wells was in London, he called on Brown to see if he had made any progress on the sale of the letters, but on this occasion Whitehouse could not be persuaded and they stayed in America.

Some items slipped into the collection almost unnoticed and by accident. In sending a group of drawings to Brantwood early in 1933, Stevens & Brown used a packing-case previously used a couple of years earlier for sending pictures to Bembridge, "thereby saving you the expense of a new one". In cleaning out the old packing-case, the men found Ruskin's sectional cone which they assumed was overlooked when the case was last used. It was duly sent to Bembridge (Bem R 112).

Equally, an album containing 33 letters from Ruskin to Louise Blandy – daughter of Ruskin's dentist, and a girl with more artistic

[Manuscript facsimile, first draft:]

Morning breaks, as I write – above – along the
Yewdale fells, and the level mists
grey beneath the rose of the moorlands, veil
the pastures by the lake shore the
the lower woods, and the sleeping village, and the long lawns
by the lake shore
Oh, that some one had told me
How little I knew, in youth, when all my
heart seemed to be set on these colours & clouds.
that appear for a little time, and then vanish
away – how little my love of them would serve
me – when, for all the silence of lawn and
wood in the dew of dawn should be completed
and all my thoughts should be of them when
by neither – I should meet more.

Brantwood. 12th February 1878

[Manuscript facsimile, fair copy:]

Morning breaks, as I write along the Yewdale Fells,
and the level mists, motionless, and grey beneath
the rose of the moorlands, veil the lower woods,
and the sleeping village, and the long lawns
by the lake-shore.
Oh, that some one had but told me, in my youth,
when all my heart seemed to be set on these
colours and clouds, that appear for a little while
and then vanish away, how little my love of them
would serve me, when the silence of lawn and
wood in the dew of morning should be completed
and all my thoughts should be of them whom
by neither, I was to meet more.

Brantwood 12th February. 1878

Ruskin's reference to the view across Coniston Lake, from the manuscript of the Epilogue to
the 1878 Turner exhibition catalogue

aspirations then talent – was offered at Sotheby's as lot 494 on 19
June 1934. Whitehouse's limit was £10 and the album was duly
bought at £8. It is now Bem B IX, and it was later to be joined in the
collection by a further group of thirteen letters which he wrote to

her (Bem L 23). Just under 60 years later a group of 77 letters to the same correspondent passed through Christie's for £5,000, but these were not bought for the collection.

Negotiations for the purchase of a substantial part of the manuscript of the 1878 Turner exhibition catalogue and some 28 letters from Ruskin to Marcus Huish were rather more protracted. Marcus Huish was the managing director of The Fine Art Society in Bond Street and he and Ruskin had a long and useful association. Their correspondence began in December 1875 – even before The Fine Art Society opened its doors – when Ruskin arranged with Huish to hold an exhibition of Turner copies made under Ruskin's direction by William Ward, another of his Working Men's College students. This exhibition led Ruskin to show a collection of his own Turner watercolours at The Fine Art Society in 1878 and to write the catalogue (which finally went to 13 editions plus a further two when the exhibition was re-staged after his death in 1900). Whitehouse had already bought the manuscript of part of the Turner catalogue at Sotheby's in 1930 (Bem MS 50/I), as Ralph Brown reminded him when offering these letters and more of the manuscript on 22 March 1934. Brown had been asked to value the material for sale by a member of the Beaumont family, who now owned it, and he put a value of £120 on it. "I do not think the price you suggest would ever be realised, or anything near it now", responded Whitehouse, who offered £20 for the material the following month. Brown thought this "rather too low", but passed on the offer to the family. Mr Beaumont said that £50 was the lowest he could accept and that it was considerably less than his father had paid for it. Brown asked Whitehouse if he had any further views – once again procrastination proved profitable – and in June he wrote to tell Brown that he had forgotten how much was suggested. By the end of June Brown explained that four members of the Beaumont family were involved and they had agreed to accept £45. On 2 August Brown reported that he had written to Henry Beaumont offering £35 – for which figure the invoice was finally drawn on 21 March and paid on 15 May 1935. The negotiations had taken fourteen months and the price had been reduced from £120 to £35 during that time!

However, Ralph Brown clearly was not too upset by Whitehouse's business methods and he had great respect for what he was doing. In April 1934, at about the time Brantwood was first opened to the public, Brown *gave* the collection a pair of watercolours by Alexander Macdonald, the first Ruskin Drawing Master at Oxford – a view of Greta Bridge in Yorkshire (Brant 746) and a second of a ruined abbey (Brant 745), thought by Brown to be Furness, but now thought to be one of the Yorkshire abbeys.

Even more protracted than the negotiations for the Beaumont manuscripts was the purchase of three drawings which Brown reported on 31 July 1934 that he had just bought from the collection of the late H. T. Butler. Sir William Rothenstein was interested in them – "but we have *not* written to him because of our arrangement to give you first refusal". The three drawings were of a cottage at Malham, probably drawn in 1875 and inscribed on the reverse by Joan Severn "Highest House in England, Malham. By Di Pa" (Bem 1380), priced at 12 guineas and described by Brown as "a real gem"; an unidentified view of Venice (*Works* Catalogue of Drawings, no. 1979), at 9 guineas, and the square tower and old houses in Rouen, 1835 (Brant 988), 10 guineas. On 31 October Whitehouse wrote: "I cannot yet decide about your three drawings from the collection of Mr Butler, but I have got the matter in hand, and will write to you soon." The original asking price was 31 guineas for the three drawings. By 10 March 1937 Brown was offering to invoice the three drawings at £21 as a special concession, and to send them to Bembridge "for you to inspect at your leisure". By return of post Brown was asked to send them for inspection and Whitehouse promised that he would "try to come to a quick decision". The "quick decision" was an offer six weeks later of £5 per drawing. Brown agreed to meet Whitehouse halfway and, in suggesting £18 for the three, said that he would also like to present to the collection "the little flower piece" (perhaps Brant 1082) which Whitehouse had recently seen at his office. Both offers were accepted on 9 May 1937 – after nearly three years of negotiations! But, to be fair, the building of the collection was not Whitehouse's only concern. At Bembridge he had just built a school chapel, substantially designed by his old Bournville acquaintance W. H. Harvey, and in early spring 1938 he was to open new refectories and a new school library.

Charles Goodspeed of Boston, Mass., had discovered Ruskin when he bought his first book in about 1887. Having lost his job in New York in the depression of 1898, he returned to Boston and established himself as a second-hand bookseller, incorporating into

Cottage at Malham – "The highest house in England", by Ruskin

his stock the Ruskin collection which he had previously built up. Over the years he always had a few customers for Ruskin, and he also rebuilt his personal collection. Because of Ruskin's interest in the education of girls and because his own daughters were graduates of Wellesley College, he eventually gave his collection of Ruskin books to that institution's library.

J. H. W. decorated the end wall of his new chapel at Bembridge with two more of Ruskin's visual aids for lectures

Partly for himself and partly for his customers, Goodspeed was one of the principal buyers at the Ruskin dispersal sales, using, as it happens, Ralph Brown as his agent. At the 1930 book sale he bought the manuscripts of *The King of the Golden River* (now in the Beinecke Library at Yale), part of *Fors Clavigera* (also at Yale), and part of the *Præterita* manuscript. He kept this last manuscript for himself; it suffered during a fire at his home, and also went to Yale eventually. He bought one or two more manuscripts in the 1931 sale; for the picture sale a couple of days later he authorised Brown to spend up to £700 on his behalf. Thus he secured many important pieces in addition to obtaining a lot of material.

Eventually, either late in 1931 or early in 1932, Goodspeed issued his Catalogue 211 – *A Catalogue of Paintings, Drawings and Manuscripts by John Ruskin*. The 108 items in the catalogue included, in addition to drawings, a group of 16 sketchbooks, a volume of early manuscript poetry, the 1831 Mineralogical Dictionary, the manuscript of *Verona and its Rivers*, part of *Deucalion*, the manuscript and proofs of *Storm Cloud of the Nineteenth Century*, and others. There were also six printed books from Ruskin's library and his celestial globe.

A copy of the catalogue was sent to Whitehouse, but he does not appear to have bought anything from it at the time. Then, in June 1933, Brown reported that there were still some 28 drawings remaining from the catalogue, some of the *Stones of Venice* worksheets and 8 of the 16 sketchbooks. Goodspeed had indicated that he would be glad to let Whitehouse have anything remaining at a special price and it would be a pleasure to him to "make the matter of profit of only secondary consideration if at all". Still Whitehouse took no action.

Then in April 1935 Goodspeed wrote directly to Whitehouse offering to send him a list of the remaining drawings, and to ship them from Boston to Bembridge for examination. A list of the more interesting items was duly sent in June. In all, there were 171 pieces, but many of them were very slight sketches of course, and the collection was offered for $1,000 (about £200). It was duly received at Bembridge and settlement was made in April 1936. Unfortunately, not all the correspondence relating to this transaction has been preserved, so it is impossible to tell whether all 171 items were shipped for inspection and retained. Judging from some of the very slight sketches in the collection that are marked with a price in dollars, I think they were all kept. Among the more interesting drawings which Goodspeed actually listed in 1935 were a water-colour of the Salute, Venice, at sunset (Bem 1630); a drawing of St Wulfran, Abbeville (almost certainly Brant 850, the striking ?1868 pencil and wash study of the top half of the church seen above the houses on that side of the marketplace); the Château de Blois, 1840 (Bem 1156); a drawing of a young Avocet, made about 1880 (Bem 1130); a street scene in Naples, 1841 (Bem 1409); a fine 1876 drawing of the Grand Canal (Bem 1622); a study of a jackal's head (Bem 1326); an interesting early drawing of Tilberthwaite Ghyll (Brant 1008); a large study of Ruskin's favourite effigy of Ilaria del Carretto by Jacapo della Quercia at Lucca (Bem 1367); and the 1835 drawing of Unterseen and the study of a pair of peacocks sur-mounted by winged lions which provided the motif for the design of the *Stones of Venice* binding (Bem 1631).

While these protracted negotiations for drawings were in progress, books and manuscripts continued to be offered to White-house. Undaunted by the problems connected with the sale of the Margaret Ruskin letters in 1933, Michelmore's offered a small group of material at the end of October 1935. There were 20 letters from Ruskin to Marcus Huish of The Fine Art Society; Michelmore had catalogued these at £35, but he offered them to Whitehouse for £25 and they seem to have been bought to join the other letters to Huish already in the collection. Another group of 20 letters from Ruskin to James Knowles, editor of the *Contemporary Review* and founder and editor of the *Nineteenth Century*, were again reduced from £35 to £25. The letters deal with, among other things, work that Ruskin was doing – or refusing to do – for his journals; they were turned down and eventually bought for £9 at Sotheby's on 17 November 1937 (Bem L 21). An important volume offered at this time by Michelmore – for £11, reduced from 12 guineas – was titled *Flora of Chamouni 1844*. It contains a collection of pressed flowers made in that year and Ruskin's extensive notes on them. This too was rejected and was bought in the next year at Sotheby's for £9. Two manuscripts – on needlework and the guild (£8, reduced from £10) – were also rejected and bought in 1937 for £1 15s. Three volumes of *Modern Painters* – I, II and IV, inscribed by Ruskin to Joan Severn – were also spurned, although the first volume subsequently came to the collection at Brantwood from the Sharp collection.

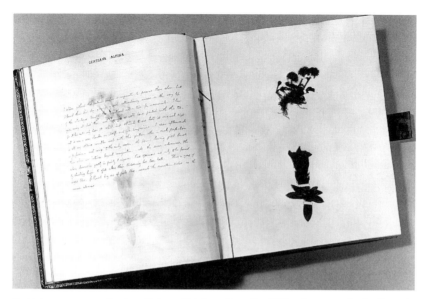

Ruskin's notes on the Gentiana Alpina, which he collected in 1844 and preserved in his *Flora of Chamouni* album

A sale at Sotheby's on 10 December 1935 contained a lot of Ruskin material, including a quantity of letters from Kate Greenaway to Ruskin, which brought more than twice Whitehouse's bid. However, for £23 5s. he was successful in buying six lots. These included the two volumes of *Friends in Council*, 1859, inscribed by Ruskin to Sarah Corlass, and 30 other unspecified volumes. Other volumes now in the collection inscribed by Ruskin to various members of the Corlass family, which may well have been included in the "30 other volumes", are H. Lee's *Legends from Fairyland*, 1860, *The Woodcutter of Lebanon*, 1854, Noyce's *Outlines of Creation*, 1858, *Flowers of many Lands, Poems and Pictures*, 1860, and Wotton's *Elements of Architecture*, 1624. Lot 369 was a copy of Ruskin's *Seven Lamps of Architecture*, 1849 (5s.), which is probably the copy in the collection inscribed "Miss Corlass with the author's sincere regards". Lots 453A and C each contained 14 letters from Ruskin to Miss Corlass, while lot 453D was six sketches and woodcuts. Robert Corlass, Sarah's father, was a wine and spirits merchant in Hull, and it is evident from the correspondence that the Ruskins and the Corlasses were family friends of long standing. Other collections of Corlass correspondence are to be found in the Huntington Library (11 letters) and the John Rylands University Library of Manchester (25 letters).

Another group of letters in the same sale was in lot 442. It cost Whitehouse £9 10s. for the two long letters (and ten drawings) from Ruskin to the Rev. Edward Clayton, a Christ Church contemporary of Ruskin's undergraduate days. This was an important early series of letters discussing theological matters.

Two items were unfortunately rejected in the summer of 1936. One was one of Ruskin's rare portraits – of Mrs Kevill-Davies, Lily of *Ethics of the Dust*. Unusually, Ruskin made three drawings of Lily. One was reproduced by Leon in his *Ruskin the Great Victorian*, 1949; there is a second in the Victoria and Albert Museum, and a third was sold at Christie's in 1985 for £14,040. It was almost certainly this last version which was not bought for the collection in 1936. The other rejected item was a significant piece of furniture that had been bought from Brantwood by A. J. Finberg, the authority on Turner. This was the Turner Cabinet from Ruskin's study, the prototype for subsequent cabinets which Ruskin had made. Although Whitehouse did not buy it, it is fortunate that the sketch diagram that Brown sent with his report was preserved.

1936 ended with another sale of importance to Ruskin collectors – the dispersal of a large part of Alexander Wedderburn's collection on 22 December; Wedderburn had died in July 1931. Whitehouse's original written instructions were for the purchase of some 30 lots; however, he and Brown met on the day before the sale and the instructions may have been changed then. In the event, he bought 19 lots for a total of £88. Some of these lots were included in the original instructions; others were not. Fortunately, there is an itemised invoice for the purchases, so in many cases we are able to know precisely what he bought.

For 10 shillings came "Turner and Ruskin 4 vols". Presumably this was Wedmore's *Turner and Ruskin*, 1900, 2 vols – perhaps a set of the de-luxe edition and a set of the ordinary – both are in the collection. The odd volume of *Unto this Last* (lot 547) which brought the seemingly high price of £2 10s. may well be the copy in the collection which has some manuscript corrections by Ruskin. "Lot 541 Fors Clavigera &c 7 vols" is difficult; it was probably a collection of miscellaneous volumes. Clearly, further interesting material was contained in "lot 542 Notes &c, a parcel" and in the portfolio of engravings which formed lot 569. The £11 paid for lot 546, "Fors &c 4 vols" probably secured Wedderburn's set of *Fors Clavigera* bound in three volumes and extensively annotated by him, together, perhaps, with his copy of *Giotto and his Works in Padua*, again annotated by him and containing his manuscript index.

Wedderburn owned a substantial number of drawings which were included in the sale and it is difficult now to identify them all. Lot 571 comprised 6 unframed drawings while the following lot was of 8 drawings by Arthur Severn and others (10s.). Lots 585 and 586 (£8 each) were 19 drawings in 13 mounts and 41 drawings in 24 mounts, both sets in cases. One of these groups could be an attractive collection of botanical studies by Ruskin. Among the drawings now in the collection and known to have belonged to Wedderburn are a study of roofs and balconies drawn between Lecco and Bergamo, given to Wedderburn by Ruskin in 1877 (Bem 1355), a striking study of an oak tree (Bem 1417) and the magnificent 1838 study of the interior of Rosslyn Chapel (Brant 987).

During the course of his travels and work, Ruskin amassed a large collection of photographs, principally of architectural interest. Wedderburn's sale (lot 587, £1) included two cases of photographs and two pages of (unidentified) manuscript. The photographs are probably part of Ruskin's collection. Also unidentified are the 20 autograph letters by Ruskin and others which comprised lot 573.

Ruskin's 1845 sketch of roofs and balconies noticed between Lecco and Bergamo, from the Wedderburn Collection

Quite a number of pieces of Ruskin manuscript were in Wedderburn's collection and these formed lots 575 to 581. They are all bound, with the circular coat of arms motif so familiar to all Ruskinians in gilt on the front board. The manuscripts bought for the collection were: lot 575, Morality in Art (Bem MS 40); lot 576, Preface to *Bibliotheca Pastorum* I (*Economist of Xenophon*, and corrected proofs) (Bem MS 41); lot 577, Valley of the Somme (Bem MS 42); lot 578, *Stones of Venice*, manuscript and drawings (Bem MS 76); and lot 581, *Love's Meinie*, ch. i. The Robin (Bem MS 43).

When collaborating with E. T. Cook on the Ruskin *Library Edition*, the editors had much of the manuscript material which was available to them typed or copied in long hand, and they then used these copies in the course of their work. Many of these volumes of transcripts are now in the Bodleian Library. Fourteen volumes were also included in this sale – lots 583 and 584 – and were bought for the collection. They are: Early Prose Writings (Bem T 16); Harry & Lucy (Bem T 17); The Puppet Show (Bem T 18); Notes on Epistle to the Romans, 2 copies (Bem T 19); Notes on Frederick William (Bem T 20); Modern Art (Bem T 21); *Modern Painters*, first draft (Bem T 22–24); Ruskin on Scott (Bem T 25); Iteriad (Bem T 26); Poems 1829–31 (Bem T 27); and Poems 1826–38 (Bem T 28).

After the successes of the previous years, 1937 and 1938 were relatively quiet. In March 1937 Whitehouse was quite excited at the prospect of the Sydney Morse sale. Morse was the husband of Juliet Tylor, one of the daughters of Alfred Tylor (1824–84), a geologist with whom Ruskin corresponded. The Morses had a large collection. They were Companions of the Guild of St George and also related by marriage to the Cunliffe family of Ambleside, who had the largest early private collection of Ruskin's drawings. After the sale, however, Brown lamented that he had been unable to succeed with any of Whitehouse's commissions because competition from the family forced up the prices. But he did buy for Whitehouse the striking watercolour of the Palazzo Minischalchi in Verona, 1845 (Bem 1658). Other than this sale, and the occasional purchase of unspecified drawings, the next high spots of the year were in November. H. Walker Thompson, a member of the staff of B. F. Stevens & Brown, who had been associated with the settlement in this country of the affairs of W. J. Linton, from whom Ruskin bought Brantwood, gave the collection two drawings by Linton made in August 1859 – Coniston village and crags from Brantwood (Bem 310) and a view looking up the lake to Coniston Head (Bem 311). Also in November Whitehouse paid Sotheby's £9 for the 20 letters from Ruskin to James Knowles and the two manuscripts relating to needlework and the guild (£1 15s.) which he had turned down when Michelmore's had offered them in October 1935.

The sale rooms seem to have been very unproductive in 1938 and in November Brown was bemoaning the fact that "there has not been much in the sales at Sotheby's". However, this period was not totally barren. In 1937–38 Whitehouse bought the very extensive collection of books by and about Ruskin made by S. W. Bush. This brought a number of elusive printed books and pamphlets into the collection, together with letters to Bush from E. T. Cook, C. E. Norton, W. G. Collingwood, Grace Allen and others (Bem L 65).

Many of the books and medieval manuscripts in Ruskin's collection were bought from Bernard Quaritch. Their association lasted from 1867 until 1888 and during that time a substantial number of letters passed between the two men. Towards the end of the nineteenth century almost all these letters were bound in two volumes. In 1938 Quaritch's daughter, Charlotte Quaritch Wrentmore, edited the letters and they were published by Bernard Quaritch Ltd. At the same time she presented the two volumes of originals to Brantwood (Bem B XVI–XVII).

Another gift at this time was a group of six pencil drawings by Thomas Bewick, whose work was greatly admired by Ruskin. These drawings of birds had been given by Ruskin to Mary Beever, Susan's sister. She in turn had passed them on to Rev. H. C. Stokes, who became the vicar of Yaverland, the neighbouring parish to Bembridge, and he gave them to the collection (Bem 83–88).

Two of six bird drawings by Thomas Bewick, formerly in the Ruskin Collection

John Ruskin: Study of Tintoretto's
Adoration, 1852

John Ruskin: Head of Solomon,
after Carpaccio, 1858

John Ruskin: Cottage near Bellinzona, 1858

John Ruskin: Old bridge at Bonneville, 1862–63

John Ruskin: View from the base of the Brezon, looking towards Geneva, 1863

John Ruskin: Walls of Lucerne, 1866

John Ruskin: Study of a dead pheasant, 1867

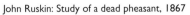

John Ruskin: Church of St Wulfran, Abbeville, 1868

John Ruskin: Abbeville
Cathedral seen from the
square, c. 1868

John Ruskin: Rose La Touche, late 1860s

John Ruskin: Brantwood, drawn for Joan Severn, 1871

John Ruskin: Roses from the dress of Flora, from Botticelli's Primavera, 1874

John Ruskin: Vineyard walk at Pozzuolo, near Lucca, 1874

Facing page:
John Ruskin: Zipporah, one of the daughters of Jethro, from Botticelli's Childhood of Moses, 1874

John Ruskin: Ferns on a rock at Brantwood, 1875

John Ruskin: North-west porch of St Mark's, Venice, 1877

John Ruskin: Picquigny, between Amiens and Abbeville, 1880

Arthur Severn: Ruskin's bedroom at Brantwood

William Ward: Bridge at St Maurice, after J. M. W. Turner

W. H. Hunt: Fruit,
formerly in Ruskin's bedroom

J. E. Millais: John Ruskin, 1853

Samuel Prout: Domo d'Ossola

T. M. Rooke: Washing-sheds at Chartres, 1885

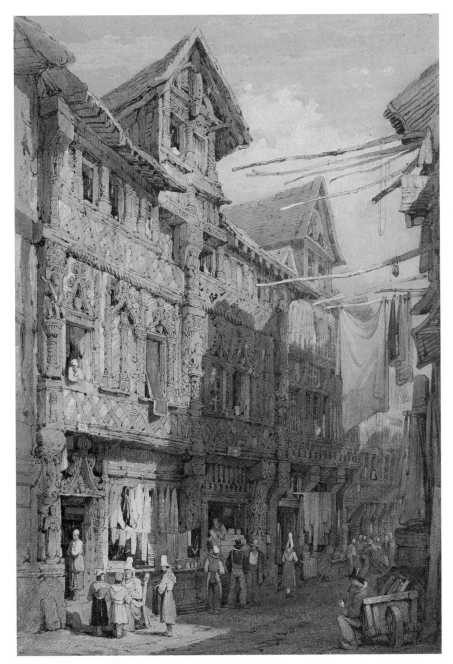

Samuel Prout: Old street in Lisieux

Edward Burne-Jones: Design for *Munera Pulveris* binding

W. G. Collingwood: Adaptation of Burne-Jones's design for *Studies in Both Arts* binding

It was at this time that Whitehouse wrote the two books which were to form the published catalogues of his collection. *Ruskin and Brantwood*, 1937, contained a summary of the history of the house and its associations, followed by a room-by-room listing and description of the contents which the visitor would see. Listed here, in addition to the pictures which Whitehouse had bought, were the portraits of John James Ruskin by George Watson and Margaret Ruskin by James Northcote. These had been bought by Mrs Atthill after the dispersal sales and placed on permanent exhibition at Brantwood. Other gifts listed in *Ruskin and Brantwood* were four watercolours given by Miss Horne.

A more substantial book, *Ruskin the Painter and his Works at Bembridge*, followed in 1938. The book opens with a 45-page essay on Ruskin, with particular emphasis on his work as an artist and on the importance of art in education. There then follows a catalogue and descriptions of the 345 drawings then in the collection at Bembridge. The volume ends with 67 half-tone reproductions of Ruskin drawings in the collection.

But the outbreak of war in September 1939 was to lead to a dramatic upheaval in the lives of Whitehouse and his collection. The first few months of the war made little impact on the life of the school; it seems that the blackout caused the most inconvenience. However, it soon became increasingly obvious that Bembridge, off the English south coast and in close proximity to the ports of Southampton and Portsmouth, was not going to be a safe place in which to pass the war years. The army also showed an interest in taking over the school's premises. In the summer term of 1940 the decision was taken to evacuate the school for the remainder of the war.

The proposed evacuation was a particular sadness for Whitehouse, for 16 May saw the 21st anniversary of the school's foundation, which would have been celebrated at the end of June at the annual Foundation Day. But the term was ended prematurely on 20 June 1940. In concluding his chapel address on the final Sunday of the term, Whitehouse said: "We will continue our school life in a new and beautiful home sacred to a great memory, and we will look forward to our reunion in the place that gave us birth."

Whitehouse had decided to evacuate the school to Brantwood. However, more detailed examination of this scheme revealed its

J. Howard Whitehouse in his study at the Waterhead Hotel, Coniston, 1942

impracticabilities. But, fortunately, at this time of crisis in the school's life, the Waterhead Hotel in Coniston came on the market. Whitehouse promptly bought the hotel and its entire contents, together with its 16 acres of ground, and it was here that the new term opened on 5 September. The accommodation had already been increased. Violet Severn had died on 7 March and on 2 September Whitehouse bought her house, No. 1 Lake Villas. "Waverley", as it was called, was to provide valuable additional dormitory space.

The packing and moving of all the school's equipment from Bembridge to Coniston was a tremendous undertaking, involving the use of 15 large railway containers. The school steward, George Houghton, supervised the greater part of the packing. During August, all the pictures in the galleries and New House were packed and transported, followed by the letters, manuscripts and more valuable printed books of the collection which remained in safety at Brantwood throughout the war.

CHAPTER IX

1940–1955

The war years, coupled with the passage of time since the Brantwood dispersal sales, saw less Ruskin material on the market and the early 1940s certainly saw fewer additions to the collection than for many years. But it also saw the addition of important works. The whole period, generally, was a difficult one for Whitehouse.

On 8 June 1940, a little over a week before the term finished prematurely at Bembridge, Whitehouse celebrated his 67th birthday. He had to contend with the wrench of the move to Coniston, wartime rationing and restrictions and the gradual erosion, through conscription, of his staff, quite apart from the general worry of the war. At Easter 1941 Ernest Baggaley, who had been on the staff since 1923 and second master for the past ten years, left to go to Wakefield Grammar School. He was succeeded as second master by T. M. Stedman, who joined Bembridge in 1929 and stayed for 40 years. In the summer of 1941 Old Bembridgian F. W. Sander, head of the junior school, was conscripted into the RAF. At the end of the same year, another Old Bembridgian, Niel Rocke, who had been bursar for a number of years, as well as being secretary of the Ruskin Society and Friends of Brantwood, left to join the Royal Navy. Arthur Windsor Richards, who with his wife had followed the Romney-Townrows as Brantwood hosts in 1937, also left about now. Inevitably, the losses of Old Bembridgians were reported. Bembridge was only a small school. By the end of the war, in 1945, 838 boys had passed through the school or were still members of it; of that number 26 had been killed – over 3 per cent of the boys Whitehouse had educated.

Although most of the business between Whitehouse and Ralph Brown had been conducted by letter, Whitehouse was in the habit of calling at his offices in Little Russell Street quite often, particularly if something significant was coming onto the market or if they had something that they wished him to see. The removal to Coniston made regular visits much more difficult, and in February

1941 Whitehouse wrote: "It seems a very long time since we met."
Much of the correspondence in 1940–41 was in relation to the
purchase of four large cartoons by Edward Burne-Jones. They had
been made as designs for windows in the English church in Berlin
and Brown had offered them to Whitehouse, suggesting that they
might be suitable for the school chapel. The cartoons depict Peace,
Justice, St George and St Michael, and they were eventually bought
and sent to Coniston after months of negotiation. They never went
into the chapel – there wouldn't have been anywhere large enough
for them.

An interesting Ruskin association item was bought in April 1941
from the dealer Raphael King. This was the diary of George
Butterworth, 1855–6 (Bem MS 35). Butterworth was a member of
Ruskin's art class at the Working Men's College and, like Allen, he
was also a carpenter. Ruskin had great hopes for Butterworth: "I had
no doubt of Mr Butterworth far surpassing me, eventually, in architectural drawing, but his career was briefly brought to a close by an
illness caused by bathing in a Welsh lake when he was heated, from
which he never recovered so as to be able to work with his full
energy again." The Ruskin Art Collection at Oxford contains a
drawing by Butterworth of Rouen Cathedral. The diary has some
interesting accounts of Ruskin at the Working Men's College as well
as accounts of many of Butterworth's conversations with him.

More manuscripts were added to the collection in August 1941.
Lot 124 in the Yates Thompson sale was 16 letters from Ruskin to
George Smith (Bem L 21), the Smith of Smith Elder, Ruskin's
publisher from 1843 until the 1870s. Later in the year, in November,
Brown offered to sell Whitehouse two very characteristic Ruskin
drawings for £10. The smaller of the two, a very economical but
effective view of the summit of Mont Blanc from his hotel window
in about 1851 (Bem 1389), was in fact given to George Butterworth
by Ruskin in 1856; in 1873 it was then "transferred" to the possession of a Mr Morrison. The larger drawing, a partially finished sepia
tree study, perhaps made at Ambleside, is inscribed by Ruskin: "Best
way of studying trees, with a view to knowledge of their leafage.
Young shoots of the Oak and Ash in Spring. J. R. 1847 (unfinished)"
(Bem 1559).

January 1942 saw Brown asking Whitehouse if he had reached a
decision about a group of four drawings, priced at 3 guineas for the

four, sent on approval in August 1940. They were eventually bought in October for £3. One was of a building which Brown thought was at Brantwood (Bem 1286), though it is now thought that it may have been a Friends' Meeting House in the Lake District. "The head of a goddess" may well be the enlarged study of a coin (Brant 900); the study of foliage and the fourth unspecified drawing are unidentified.

May and June 1942 saw Brown making bulk purchases of books for Whitehouse at Hodgson's. These were probably intended for the school library. One lot of 200 volumes for £7 and another of 50 volumes for £1 8s. in May were followed in June by 650 volumes and 8 parcels of books for £20 7s. In all, Brown had to arrange for the shipment of almost a ton of books to Coniston!

During the course of these transactions Brown mentioned to Whitehouse that he had noticed Ruskin's 1858 drawing of "a cottage near Bellinzona" being described in an old *Magazine of Art* as belonging to M. H. Spielmann. This drawing had been given to Spielmann by Ruskin. Brown asked if he should approach Spielmann to ask if he would sell the drawing to Whitehouse, and it was eventually added to the collection (Bem 1148).

Both Whitehouse and Brown were sceptical about the origins of the important watercolour which Brown sent to Coniston in June 1942. It *is* unlike most Ruskin watercolours, but the authentication on it, signed by Ruskin's valet Frederick Crawley, finally tipped the scales and fortunately Whitehouse kept it. It is a study of Mount Pilatus (Bem 1437), done in 1835 in the style of Copley Fielding. Almost all the 1935 pencil drawings were worked up into pen and ink drawings to illustrate Ruskin's poetical account of the tour. But in the case of *this* view, Ruskin worked up his sketch (also in the collection, Bem 1435) into a watercolour, using all the tricks and mannerisms taught by his master. The calm lake is whipped up into a storm, with rain, a dramatically dead tree on the little promontory in the foreground, and the Gothic mountain towering in the background. Four other Copley Fielding-style watercolours from the Sharp collection are now also at Brantwood.

Other drawings, about which Whitehouse and Brown had no doubts, were the street scene in Genoa drawn on 2 November 1840 (Bem 1295), bought at the end of October, and the "old buildings" and view of Geneva from the Rhône, 1846 (Bem 1290), which came from Christie's on 18 December for £22 1s. As it happens, their confidence may have been misplaced. John Hayman points out that there is an almost identical view of Geneva in the Huntington Library which is inscribed by Ruskin. Examples *are* known of Ruskin making copies of his own drawings but, in the case of the present drawing, Cook and Wedderburn note in their Catalogue of Drawings (No. 762) that a copy by Miss Harrison exists. In view of the Ruskin inscription on the Huntington version and the *lack* of it on the Bembridge version, one is reluctantly forced to the conclusion that the Bembridge version is Miss Harrison's copy – but she was a *very* good copyist.

Hoping to secure Brantwood's future, Whitehouse had for some time been having discussions with friends at Oxford. The outcome of the talks was that in November 1942 the university accepted the gift of Brantwood, which it would maintain as a memorial to Ruskin and as a place to which the university could send reading parties. However, the university had second thoughts and wished to return the gift. Since a trust had been created, it took several years and many legal fees before the gift was finally returned to Whitehouse's Education Trust, so that it could be managed by its own group of Brantwood Trustees.

1 June of the next year saw the purchase at Sotheby's of lots 239–244, some fragmentary Ruskin manuscripts – the two-and-a-half-page preface to *The Story of Ida* (Bem MS 51/G), three pages intended for *Deucalion* (Bem MS 51/H), ten and a half pages of *Love's Meinie* (Bem MS 50/H), twelve pages of *Proserpina* (Bem MS 51/J), two pages of comments on "A Familiar Colloquy" by W. H. Mallock (Bem MS 51/I) and a page of the *Bible of Amiens* manuscript – all for £17 10s.

In the following month Sotheby's sold the watercolour and ink sketch of Pisa with the campanile of San Nicola, drawn on 13 May 1845 in Ruskin's sketch-book (Bem 1445). At the same time Brown sent four pencil sketches of architectural details at Genoa (Bem 1291 and 1292 and two others which are unidentified). "The Garden of the Capucins" drawing (Bem 1288) followed a few days later and, on 5 October, lot 24 was a watercolour of Ruskin's favourite Castelbarco Tomb drawn in Verona in 1869 (Bem 1649).

In December Brown wrote to say that, at a few hours' notice, he had been warned that two Ruskin drawings "were sandwiched amongst a lot of valueless amateur drawings" in a Red Cross sale at

Robinson & Foster's Rooms in St James's. He attended the sale and bought two little 1854 drawings of Thun on blue paper in one mount (Bem 1546–1547), a drawing of a convent at Sallenches, a square building with a round tower at one end which had caught Ruskin's attention in 1856 (Bem 1484), and a drawing of the towers of the abbey at Baden in Switzerland (Bem 1135), made in 1859 and inscribed by Ruskin: "Very careful half an hour, meant to be gone on with … these roofs are drawn with my most delicate care, but were grievously rubbed before I got them mounted." All four drawings had been bought by Dr J. J. Brigg over 30 years before for a total of £40 15s.; Brown secured them for £22 13s. 6d. and, because it was a sale in aid of the Red Cross, he did not charge his usual commission.

Additions to the collection seem to have been few in 1944, or Whitehouse's filing system, which at best was erratic, had almost totally collapsed due to understaffing. His correspondence with Brown shows that he was again making bulk purchases of books for the school library – and for his own. He had always been interested in boys' literature and among many other books bought about now was a long run of the *Boys' Own Paper*. He did buy two drawings by T. M. Rooke in June – studies at Fécamp (Bem 436) and "Mosley" (actually Morlaix, Bem 440).

A sale at Sotheby's at the end of July brought a set of *Edwin Drood* in the original parts; more importantly, lot 259 was 16 letters from Ruskin to the Rev. Charles Chapman, vicar of Coniston (£9 10s., Bem L 23), and lot 23 was even more desirable. It was a box containing a first edition of *Sesame & Lilies*, with two drawings by Burne-Jones contained in a pocket. In 1863 Ruskin had plans for producing a fine edition of *Munera Pulveris*, lavishly illustrated after designs by Burne-Jones. The essays of this title originally appeared in *Frazer's Magazine* and the plans for the book were interrupted by the death of Ruskin's father in 1864. The essays eventually appeared in book form in 1872, but without the Burne-Jones embellishments.

Burne-Jones only seems to have finished the design for the binding (Bem 138), one of the two designs in the *Sesame* box. The design was never used for *Munera Pulveris*, but in 1895 it was adapted by W. G. Collingwood as the binding for his *Studies in Both Arts*. It was redrawn again in 1975 as the cover design for the Arts Council's Burne-Jones exhibition catalogue. The other design in the box (Bem 139) was Burne-Jones's sketch for a title page for Ruskin's

Sesame and Lilies. Again, this was never used for its intended purpose and was never published until it appeared as the frontispiece to vol. XVIII of the *Library Edition*.

Early in 1945 Brown offered Whitehouse a group of 47 letters from Ruskin to the bookseller F. S. Ellis and his partner, from whom Ruskin had bought many books and manuscripts. The offer also included, for the asking price of £30, 15 letters from Joan and Arthur Severn to various correspondents. Whitehouse declined the offer, saying that the letters were in poor condition, of little interest, and overpriced.

However, he showed more interest in the W. B. Slater sale at Hodgson's on 22 February. Slater had been a lifelong friend of Thomas J. Wise, whose activities as a forger are now well known. He had been a witness at Wise's second marriage and was one of the executors of his will who arranged the sale of Wise's Ashley Library to the British Museum. Slater was also a book collector. The two-day sale of his library realised in excess of £5,000; it contained an exceptional number of Wise editions, at that time the largest group ever to have appeared on the market.

By this time Whitehouse already owned multiple copies of most of Wise's Ruskin productions. But he bought three lots in the Slater

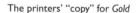
Burne-Jones's design for the *Sesame and Lilies* title page

The printers' "copy" for *Gold*

sale. Lot 298, for £17, was a group of 30 letters from Ruskin to F. J. Furnivall (Bem L 17), some of which certainly appeared in Wise's edition of *Letters from John Ruskin to Frederick J. Furnivall, M.A.*, 1897; lot 299 contained 32 letters from Ruskin to Rossetti, Butler, Dallas and Crawley. Perhaps the most interesting lot of the three was lot 297, bought for £28. This contained a sketch-book (unidentified) and copies of two letters from F. D. Maurice to F. J. Furnivall (one certified by Wise as being in Furnivall's hand) and two letters from Maurice to Ruskin. The letters had originally been published by Wise as an article in *Literary Anecdotes*, and the type was subsequently reimposed and used to print the limited edition of *John Ruskin and Frederick Denison Maurice on "Notes on the Construction of Sheepfolds"*, 1896 (Bem MS 50/A). Also included in this lot was the printer's copy for Ruskin's *Gold*, edited by H. Buxton Forman and published by Wise in 1891 (Bem MS 50/B). Attached to the copy is a letter from Forman to Slater saying that he was sending it to him at Wise's suggestion.

Of course, the greatest excitement of 1945 was the return to Bembridge. The end of the war in Europe and the de-requisitioning of the school site by the army made this possible. The last military unit had left the school grounds in the early summer of 1944. Almost immediately, the work of repairing the devastation left by four years of army occupation was put in hand and the huge task of packing everything at Coniston for the return to Bembridge began. Eventually the school was habitable (although work continued for many months), and the autumn term of 1945 opened at Bembridge on 3 October. Among the new boys joining the school in that interesting term was the incipient book and picture collector J. S. Dearden!

The years immediately following the return to Bembridge were also not very productive for the collection, although there were a few useful additions. A Ruskin drawing and the 1801 Turner drawing of Stirling Castle (Bem 577), formerly in Norton's collection, came from Sir Michael Sadler's sale in October 1946, while a sale at Sotheby's in the following month produced the 1837 drawing of cottages at Troutbeck (Brant 1013) and the slightly out-of-character view of Bristol, with shipping on the Avon and St Mary Radcliff in the background (Bem 1178), which may date from 1839, but almost certainly not 1833 as suggested by Cook and Wedderburn.

Chronologically and stylistically it does not seem right, despite being authenticated by Joan Severn, and I am inclined to doubt that this work was done by Ruskin. However, there seems little doubt that the distant view of Oxford (Bem 1421) bought at Sotheby's in May 1946 dates from Ruskin's time as an undergraduate.

A single lot from Sotheby's (lot 46, 17 December 1946) brought a further quantity of manuscript material to Bembridge – the manuscript index to *Fors Clavigera* 1 & 2 (Bem 50/G), together with two letters to Mrs A. W. Hunt and one from her about the index, and 28 letters from Ruskin and his father and Joan Severn to Coventry Patmore and Bertha (Bem L 14). A mis-catalogued item at Sotheby's on 10 January 1947 was not allowed to slip through the net. Catalogued as "Scenes from the life of Christ by John Ruskin in emulation of an early missal", the trade was not misled, and the underbidder was a continental dealer in manuscripts and incunabula. The lot, which had previously been in Hugh Walpole's collection, is an awful example of Ruskin dismembering his medieval manuscripts. It comprises one large miniature surrounded by 20 smaller arched-top miniatures cut from a French *Book of Hours* of about 1430. These are all "arranged" by Ruskin and pasted onto a group

A series of medieval miniatures cut up and "arranged" by Ruskin

of strips of marginal decoration cut from an ? Italian sixteenth-century *Gradual*. All these are pasted onto a piece of heavy card and mounted and framed (Bem 194).

Later that year Whitehouse acquired two volumes of *Præterita* from the Harmsworth sale, each signed on the fly leaf by C. L. Dodgson. A month later a drawing for *The Stones of Venice* from the S. C. Cockerell/Emery Walker collection (unidentified) and a view near Bellinzona (also unidentified) were bought at Sotheby's and Christie's respectively.

The publication in January 1948 of Sir William James's book *The Order of Release* caused a considerable stir in the Ruskin world. The title is taken from a painting by Millais. The book's subject was Ruskin's marriage, its breakdown and his wife's subsequent marriage to Millais. Admiral James was in fact their grandson. The sensational story attracted the attention of the popular press and the book was widely reviewed. It *was* biased in favour of Effie, and the admiral's editorial practice was suspect. Whitehouse took him to task in the review which he wrote for *John o'London's Weekly*, describing it as a painful book to read and one which he felt should not have been published. Whitehouse also spoke out against the book – at length – in his speech at the annual luncheon of the Ruskin Society on 8 February, as did other speakers – Sir Arthur Salter M.P. and J. W. Robertson Scott, the editor of *The Manchester Guardian*. This, of course, kept the press coverage and the correspondence active.

Prompted by this furore, Whitehouse received a letter from Alister Wedderburn, son of the co-editor of the *Library Edition*. At the time of the annulment of his marriage in 1854, Ruskin had written a statement in which he outlined the facts of his marriage. The annulment was never contested and thus Ruskin's statement was never used. It remained in his solicitor's hands, being passed on from partner to successive partner through the years until, in 1924, needing money, Mrs Veitch, the widow of a later owner, sold the document. It was bought by Effie Millais' brother, Sir Albert Gray, who intended to destroy it. Happily the document was known to Alexander Wedderburn, Ruskin's surviving literary executor. Following lengthy correspondence, Gray relinquished the document to Wedderburn, but not before he had copied the statement. After the death of his widow in 1938 this copy was given to the Bodleian

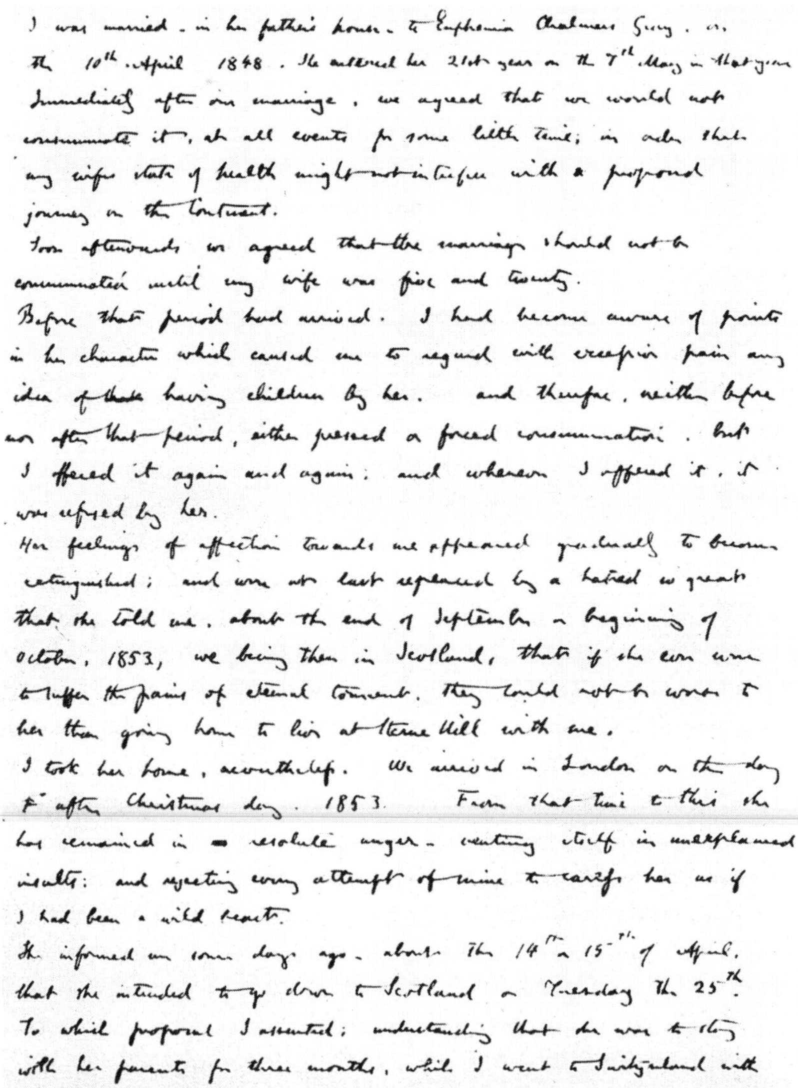
I was married – in her father's house – to Euphemia Chalmers Gray – on
the 10th April 1848. She entered her 21st year on the 7th May in that year.
Immediately after our marriage, we agreed that we would not
consummate it, at all events for some little time; in order that
my wife's state of health might not interfere with a proposed
journey on the Continent.
Soon afterwards we agreed that the marriage should not be
consummated until my wife was five and twenty.
Before that period had arrived. I had become aware of points
in her character which caused me to regard with excessive pain any
idea of there having children by her. and therefore, neither before
nor after that period, either pressed a forced consummation: but
I offered it again and again: and whenever I offered it, it
was refused by her.
Her feelings of affection towards me appeared gradually to become
extinguished; and were at last replaced by a hatred so great
that she told me, about the end of September or beginning of
October, 1853, we being then in Scotland, that if she were
to suffer the pains of eternal torment, they could not be worse to
her than going home to live at Herne Hill with me.
I took her home, nevertheless. We arrived in London on the day
after Christmas day. 1853. From that time to this she
has remained in a resolute anger – venting itself in unexplained
insults: and rejecting every attempt of mine to caress her as if
I had been a wild beast.
She informed me some days ago – about the 14th or 15th of April,
that she intended to go down to Scotland on Tuesday the 25th.
To which proposal I assented; understanding that she was to stay
with her parents for three months, while I went to Switzerland with
my father and mother. I saw her depart by the railway at ½ past 9
on Tuesday morning. and was surprised to receive the citation to
court the same afternoon.

Part of Ruskin's statement regarding his marriage

Library, with the proviso that it could not be published for 30 years. After Alexander Wedderburn's death and the dispersal of the bulk of his Ruskin collection, the statement was retained by his family. Alister Wedderburn wrote to Whitehouse in 1948 to say that, in his opinion, the time had come for the statement to be published. He gave all of the papers to Whitehouse on condition that he published the statement in Ruskin's defence. This Whitehouse duly did in his book, *Vindication of Ruskin*, which was eventually published in July 1950.

By 1948 I had begun to take some interest in Ruskin and, knowing that Whitehouse was writing a book in his defence, I transcribed for him some passages from Ruskin's diary for 1853 relating to the painting of the Glenfinlas portrait. I clearly remember Whitehouse returning from London with the papers that Wedderburn had given him, and his excitement and enthusiasm at really having the material to present the Ruskin version of the marriage fiasco.

The papers which he brought back with him not only included Ruskin's statement to his proctor (Bem MS 66); there was also a substantial file (Bem L 67) of supporting and allied material. Here is correspondence between Alexander Wedderburn, Greville Macdonald and Mrs Hotham (Rose La Touche's niece) about possible references to Rose in Macdonald's proposed biography of his parents; between Wedderburn and Clement Shorter and T. J. Wise on the pamphlet *An Ill-Assorted Marriage*, issued in 1915 by Shorter in a limited edition of 25 copies; and between Wedderburn and Sir Albert Gray in 1904, with corrected proofs, on how the Ruskin–Effie separation should be treated in volume XII of the *Library Edition*. There are notes by Cook and Wedderburn on Ruskin's marriage, with transcripts from his diary and from the Commissary Court Proceedings, and correspondence between Wedderburn and Mrs Veitch and her late husband's firm as well as Mackrell & Ward (Ruskin's solicitors). Here too are the letters between Wedderburn and Gray leading to Wedderburn's recovery of the statement. Finally, there is an exchange of letters in 1946 between Alister Wedderburn and Sir William James, in which Wedderburn urges him to leave well alone in relation to the old story of Ruskin's marriage. The whole file shows how assiduously the Wedderburns, father and son, strove to protect Ruskin's good name.

It seems possible that in about 1948 the Wedderburns may also have parted with other Ruskin material. I remember drawing Whitehouse's attention to 15 volumes of Cook and Wedderburn transcripts from Ruskin's diaries which were offered for sale in one of John Grant's catalogues (Bem T 2–25). Drawings from the

Wedderburn collection also came onto the market at this time. In May 1948 Whitehouse bought the drawing of a branch against a blue sky which was a second study for "The Dryad's Waywardness" of *Modern Painters* V (Bem 1415), and in October 1949 he bought three more tree studies, an aspen (not *the* Fontainebleau aspen!) against a blue sky (Bem 1125), and an oak (Bem 1417) and a lime tree (Bem 1358), which had also probably been in Wedderburn's collection. Another ex-Wedderburn drawing also acquired in October 1949 is the impressive study, drawn in 1862–3, of the old bridge at Bonneville (Bem 1158).

Meanwhile, in January 1948, one of Ruskin's several designs for windows for the Oxford Museum (Bem 1423) came to Bembridge from the collection of Colin Deane, the grandson of Sir Thomas Deane, of Deane, Woodward and Deane, who designed the museum. Ruskin was much involved with the building and drew at least a dozen different ideas for windows there.

Ruskin's study for an etching of Fribourg, made in 1856 as part of his projected series of illustrations of Swiss history (Bem 1284), had joined the collection in July 1948. A fine and important drawing in which Ruskin recorded the unrestored part of the façade of the Ca' d'Oro in Venice in 1845 came to Bembridge from the Harmsworth collection in June 1949 (Bem 1590).

Charles Augustus Howell was a colourful character who was associated in his time with many of the Pre-Raphaelites and their friends – "That Polecat Howell", Swinburne (whose literary agent he was for a while) called him. Graham Robertson wrote that "he had in his time been almost everybody's bosom friend and usually their private secretary". Rossetti wrote of him:

> There's a Portuguese person named Howell
> Who lays on his lies with a trowel:
>   Should he give over lying
>   'Twill be when he's dying
> For living is lying with Howell.

One evening after dinner, when Howell had been telling some of his tales, Ruskin's mother, who stood no nonsense, threw down her knitting and asked: "How can you sit there and listen to such a pack of lies?" Howell was Ruskin's private secretary in the mid-1860s; his principal activity seems to have been to help Ruskin in his

Fribourg, one of the drawings made in 1856 by Ruskin for his projected Swiss history

philanthropic activities. But, as Graham Robertson also observed, the secretaryships almost always came to an abrupt end owing to financial complications.

M. H. Spielmann had a series of 65 letters from Ruskin to Howell (and one to Rossetti) (Bem B I), and these were added to the collection from a sale at Sotheby's on 12 December 1949 where lots 790–955 were all items of Spielmann's. With the exception of a small, unidentified group of letters in 1952, this collection of letters to Howell seems to be the last set of manuscripts that Whitehouse bought.

However, pictures continued to arrive at Bembridge: at the end of 1949 there was a small 1835 drawing of the Gardener's Cottage, Tulse Hill (Bem 1289), and, more importantly, in May 1950 the drawing which Ruskin made in 1866 of the cemetery at Neuchâtel with the grave of Lady Trevelyan. Lady Trevelyan had died there while on tour with her husband and Ruskin, her niece Constance Hilliard and Joan Agnew. Ruskin made the drawing, with the grave in the foreground, for Sir Walter. It was bought from the Trevelyan collection.

Whitehouse had long owned several drawings by T. M. Rooke, including the magnificent Washing-Sheds at Chartres (Brant 771) which belonged to Ruskin. Rooke was born in 1842 and in 1869 he became Burne-Jones's assistant. He was almost certainly introduced to Ruskin by Burne-Jones and in 1879 Ruskin commissioned him to make studies of mosaics in St Mark's, Venice, which were in the process of "restoration". Thereafter he frequently worked for Ruskin or the Guild of St George, making many detailed architectural studies. He died in his 100th year in 1942. Whitehouse had met and corresponded with Rooke. He also knew Rooke's son Noel, who was a painter, wood engraver and book decorator – and a much respected teacher at the Central School of Arts and Crafts. In December 1950 Whitehouse was given the opportunity to select a group of watercolours by Rooke from the family collection. Of the 24 that he chose, the family wished to retain 7, but he was offered instead a large interior of Durham Cathedral and a medium-sized drawing of Queen Bertha's staircase at Chartres (about which Ruskin had written), making 19 in all. These were:

"Large"

Bourges, east end, 1899 (Bem 428)
Cremona, west front (Bem 432)
Tournus, 1926 (Bem 449)
Lisieux, church of St Jacques, 1891 (Bem 437)
St Bartholomew, Smithfield, 1920 (Bem 445)
Tewkesbury, east end (Bem 448)
Durham, 1913 (Bem 433)

"Medium"

Troyes, St Jean de, in 1890, 1924 (Bem 450)
Monastier, church, 1908 (Bem 439)
Faulin, 1905 (Bem 434 or 435)
Tewkesbury, north-west (Bem 447)
Romsey, south-east (Bem 441)
Romsey, east
Westminster, north aisle, 1924 (Bem 453)
Westminster, north-aisle chapels, 1922 (Bem 452)
Chartres, Queen Bertha's staircase (untraced)

"Small"

Monastier, town cross, 1908 (Bem 438)
Bourges, tower, 1889 (Bem 429)
Rye, Mermaid Street, 1889 (Bem 444).

The price agreed for the 19 watercolours was £100. The selected drawings were included in the T. M. Rooke exhibition at the R.I.B.A. in May 1951, before being brought down to Bembridge.

Another large collection of drawings, this time by Ruskin, came in March 1951. These were all drawings from the collection of Sara Anderson, once Ruskin's secretary. Most of them had been given to her by Ruskin himself. The collection had been bought privately by Brown and he offered Whitehouse the first refusal – at £30 "absolute lowest"! Interestingly, there was a preponderance of early drawings in this group. Of particular importance is the partly finished drawing of Hampton Court (Bem 1312), "copy from Charles Runciman", as Ruskin had inscribed it in 1885. Runciman was Ruskin's drawing master and this lesson drawing was copied from Runciman in 1833 or 1834. From the 1837 tour to northern England came the drawing of the window in the Infirmary Chapel at Furness Abbey (Bem 1287), while the Scottish tour of the following year is represented by two drawings of St Anthony's Chapel, Edinburgh (Bem 1240 and 1241). Also from Edinburgh there is a drawing of Salisbury Crags (Bem 1242). There is a little watercolour study of a cockle shell (Bem 1510), a study of a wild flower with foliage (unidentified), a beautiful little ink and wash study of Fribourg, 1856 (Bem 1285), and a copy of two girls and a dog after Veronese's The Pilgrims of Emmaus (Bem 1554). The collection also included a sepia study of a ruin in a landscape by Arthur Severn, a couple of photographs and an engraving.

In May 1951 Brown offered Whitehouse a study of Mount Pilatus (Bem 1436), drawn in grey washes in 1846 and expertly showing the modelling of the mountain. The inscription shows that Arthur Severn sold Ruskin's drawings in his lifetime: "Bought of Mr Arthur Severn at Brantwood, June 1898 by my friend Mr C. E. Matthews."

Four days later, at Christie's, Brown paid 34 guineas for two very desirable portraits by Millais from the Trevelyan collection. The head and shoulders of Ruskin (Bem 356) was drawn by Millais at Wallington, the Trevelyans' house in Northumberland, in June 1853 for Lady Trevelyan, during the Ruskins' and Millais' visit to the house while *en route* to Glenfinlas. The second portrait is of Ruskin's lifelong friend Sir Henry Acland (Bem 355). Acland was staying in Edinburgh in the summer of 1853 and joined the party at Glenfinlas between 25 July and 1 August. Millais found him "an amiable man", and that was probably when this portrait was drawn.

Brown was commissioned to buy a mixed lot at Sotheby's on 11 March 1952 which cost £22 and comprised four Ruskin letters, one from Carlyle, some from Burne-Jones and Severn, and pamphlets, cuttings and two small Ruskin sketches. Whitehouse was disappointed. "I am very sorry that I asked you to buy lot 182. I find the contents almost valueless. Except for the two small drawings by Ruskin the rest of the contents are almost valueless. The bulk of them are advertisements for the Library Edition. But I do not blame you in the matter. I think the catalogue was misleading by including so much rubbish." Ultimately, he kept the two small unidentified drawings and returned the rest. The material had come from the Morse collection and seems to have been put back into Sotheby's.

Whitehouse celebrated his eightieth birthday on 8 June 1953. He was still running Bembridge School, but he was increasingly plagued by ill-health. As was his custom, he was one of the umpires when the Old Bembridgians XI played the school in July. Unhappily, during the course of the match he was struck in the left eye by a ball being returned from the boundary. He lost the sight of the eye and it took him a long time to recover from the shock of the accident – in fact, he never really recovered, despite writing to Brown on 27 January 1954: "The reason I have not written is that I have only just recovered from an illness."

1954, in fact, was to see the end of Whitehouse's career as a collector – but not before he had added a further number of worthwhile drawings to his collection. A little watercolour of a slave boat (Bem 422) by David Roberts came from a sale on 26 February. There was an 1837 Ruskin drawing in the sale which was probably the impressive study of a street in Derby with the tower of what is now Derby Cathedral (Bem 1229).

On 5 March Brown reported that he had recently acquired a small pen and ink profile sketch of Ruskin by T. Henderson (Bem 236), the date of which he mistook for 12 December 1884. He offered it to Whitehouse for 2 guineas and the offer was duly accepted. The year of the sketch must in fact be 1864, not 1884. On 12 December 1864 Ruskin was in Manchester to deliver his *Sesame and Lilies* lectures. The first lecture, "On Kings' Treasuries", was delivered on 6 December, and the second, "On Queens' Gardens", on 14 December. During the visit to Manchester Ruskin also addressed the boys of the Manchester Grammar School, probably on 7 December. It seems likely that Henderson had been in Ruskin's audience on 6 or 7 December and had seen Ruskin there, before he drew this little portrait. On the 12th, the day the sketch was made, Ruskin was actually at Winnington, the school near Northwich in which he took an interest.

Whitehouse bought his last drawing on 3 November 1954 at Sotheby's. It is of the west end of Peterborough Cathedral seen from the cloisters (Bem 1433), a drawing which Ruskin made on his 1837 tour of England. It is a fine example of his work at that time, and one of the few of his own drawings which he hung in his own home. It had later belonged to the wife of Canon Rawnsley, herself the daughter of a bishop of Peterborough. Brown had warned Whitehouse of the impending sale on 28 October, and he described the lot: "I have seen the drawing which is a typical example of Ruskin's work in that medium. Probably it could be bought for £16 to £20. Please let me know if you would like us to act for you." Too unwell to reply personally, he had the bursar, Niel Rocke, reply on his behalf. The reply is a testament to the trust which Whitehouse placed in Brown's reliability as an agent: "I have your letter of 28 October addressed to Mr Whitehouse. He has been very unwell lately and although he is now a little better again, he is not writing letters. I read him your letter and he said would I tell you that he left the matter entirely to you."

John Howard Whitehouse died ten months later, on 28 September 1955. His ashes were buried in the school chapel at Bembridge which he had built twenty years earlier. His memorial service was held at St Margaret's, Westminster, on 16 December. In his address, the Rev. Mervyn Stockwood, Old Bembridgian and later Bishop of Southwark, paid eloquent tribute to Whitehouse:

> He was a bold pioneer in the field of education ... it is no exaggeration to say that there is scarcely a school-boy in the country who does not owe something to his influence ... In the best and fullest sense of the word, Howard Whitehouse was a liberal ... he valued individual worth, reverenced individuality and encouraged individualism ... although he gave of his best to his School, he was not parochial ... his devotion to Ruskin ... indicate a man with broad vision and a large heart.

Whitehouse was mourned by many and is still well remembered. His work for education at Bembridge School and elsewhere, and his devotion to Ruskin, will secure him a small place in history.

CHAPTER X

1955–1969

Whitehouse had striven throughout his life to keep the name and teaching of Ruskin alive. He had written, lectured and collected throughout a period when there was little interest in his idol. Other than his own books, few others had been published. There had been Amabel Williams Ellis's *John Ruskin*, 1928, David Larg's *John Ruskin*, 1932, Wilenski's controversial *John Ruskin, an Introduction to Further Study of his Life and Work*, 1933, and Peter Quennell's *John Ruskin, the Portrait of a Prophet*, 1949.

That same year, 1949, saw the publication of Derrick Leon's *Ruskin the Great Victorian*. This was the first biography since Collingwood and Cook and Wedderburn to make use of previously unpublished material and, as such, it must be seen as marking the beginning of a new era in Ruskin scholarship. Leon used material in the Beinecke Library at Yale as well as material in private hands – Mrs Angeli, Mrs Detmar Blow, Sir Sidney Cockerell, Charles Goodspeed, Mrs Michael Joseph, Dr Greville Macdonald, Sir Ralph Millais, and others – but, as far as I can trace, he made no attempt to communicate with Whitehouse or to use material at Bembridge.

Others did, however. Helen Viljoen in New York had been studying Ruskin since the early 1920s. She had worked at Brantwood in 1929, before the collection was wholly dispersed, and at the end of 1949 or the beginning of 1950 she wrote to Whitehouse with queries relating to the Ruskin diaries. Whitehouse either misunderstood her request or did not have time to answer her queries, and she did not receive a very productive reply. In 1953 Brown drew Whitehouse's attention to Viljoen's request, published in *The Book Collector*, for material relating to the Bowerswell papers. A year later Brown told Whitehouse that Dr Margaret Spence had been enquiring about the Ruskin–Somerscales correspondence (Bem L 16), but by this stage of his life and the condition of his health, Whitehouse did not feel inclined to follow up the enquiry, and her series of papers published between 1957 and 1961 in the *Rylands Bulletin* were written without reference to Bembridge material, as was her book, *Dearest Mama Talbot*, 1966. In the same way, Bradley's *Ruskin's Letters from Venice 1851–1852* were edited in isolation, because, as he observed: "the letters written during 1851–52 by the older man [Ruskin's father] to his son are not accessible ..."

Unfortunately, the one person who did persuade Whitehouse to make material available was Joan Evans. In the early 1950s Whitehouse agreed to her editing the *Diaries*; although his name appears with hers on the title pages as joint editor, he took no active part in the venture, other than making the manuscripts and transcripts available to her. In her preface she said that Whitehouse had always hoped to write such a piece himself, and she pointed out that her own biographical introduction to the diaries had grown into her *John Ruskin*, 1954. Whitehouse was bitterly disappointed when he received his copy of her book, thinking that the packet was going to contain the first volume of the *Diaries* – which in fact was not published until the year after his death.

After Whitehouse's death, the pattern of activities at Bembridge changed. The school was increased in size in order to make it more economically viable and, while the school continued to maintain the collection, there was very little financial support available for it. Whitehouse's successor as chairman of Education Trust Ltd. was R. G. Lloyd, a successful barrister and Q.C., who had been a member of the teaching staff at Bembridge in the early 1930s. He and his wife did their utmost to continue to run the school, the collection and Brantwood as they thought Whitehouse would have wished, and their financial support of Brantwood in particular enabled it to survive as a Ruskin memorial.

This was a transitional stage for the collection. In 1956, partly to establish that the collection belonged to Education Trust Ltd., and partly to raise funds to pay some Whitehouse bequests, some items were sold at Sotheby's. The sale of 11 December included as lot 23 a fifteenth-century Flemish manuscript, *Book of Devotions*, and Ruskin's *Salisbury Missal* (lot 24), a fifteenth-century northern French manuscript. Both of these manuscripts had been bought by Whitehouse from Arthur Severn. The same sale included the early fifteenth-century English *Flaunden Missal* (lot 22), an illuminated manuscript which did not have a Ruskin provenance. A few days later, on 18 December, the sale contained as lot 400 the illuminated

Book of Hours printed in Paris by Simon Vostre in the early years of the sixteenth century. This book had also come from the Ruskin collection, through Severn.

In the early spring of 1957 I returned to my home near Barrow-in-Furness from London, where I had lived for a couple of years. During the Easter weekend I visited Brantwood for tea with the Lloyds, who were staying there. Conversation turned to Bembridge, and Mr Lloyd asked if I knew of anyone who could sort all of Whitehouse's personal papers, which were still there. I said I would do it, and in May I returned to Bembridge.

The Upper Gallery was still as Whitehouse had left it, with the walls lined with pictures by Ruskin and others, and the drawers and cupboards stuffed with unsorted and uncatalogued letters and manuscripts. The Lower Gallery, which I later renamed "The Warden's Library", was in a totally unusable state. An odd growth of shelves had surrounded and linked those that had been put in when the galleries were built. These all housed the Ruskin books and much other miscellaneous printed matter, which spilled over onto the large oak tables in the room. Almost all the floor space was occupied by boxes of filed or unfiled papers. Eventually, the room was refurbished and put into a usable state. The Whitehouse papers were sorted, but remain largely uncatalogued because events took over! It was clear to both Lloyd and myself that it was necessary to have someone here permanently to look after the collection, but finance was the problem. However, I knew that Tom Stedman, the second master, who had taught printing (among many other subjects) since the 1930s, wanted to give up that time-consuming part of his activities. When I offered to divide my time between caring for the collection and teaching printing, my position was made permanent. I had to learn my Ruskin and catalogue the collection in order to deal with the inquiries which were already beginning to arrive as a result of increasing interest in Ruskin. One of the first things I had to do was to look for any references to the footpaths at Brantwood, of interest to Sam Brown in Maryland, who was working on the proofs of *Præterita*.

It was soon after my arrival at Bembridge that I was instrumental in making some important additions to the collection. For some time my parents had known F. J. Sharp of Barrow-in-Furness, a craftsman in wood. About 1947 Sharp bought from my father a small electric motor to power one of his lathes. During the course of conversation Sharp learned that I was at school at Bembridge; assuming, I suppose not unnaturally, that I must therefore be interested in Ruskin, it was arranged that my mother and I would visit him in Westgate Road, where he lodged with Mrs Holmes. I should have taken more notice of what he showed me! I told Whitehouse about Sharp's Ruskin collection and he expressed interest. In the late 1940s Whitehouse used to travel north by sleeper from Euston to Barrow, where we would meet him. Having taken him home for breakfast, we would drive him to Brantwood for the day, then home again for dinner, before putting him on the sleeper again for the return to Bembridge. On one of these fleeting visits, time was made to take him to meet Sharp and see his collection. It was with increasing amazement and jealousy that Whitehouse saw the things that Sharp had produced. Any number of rooms at Brantwood were immediately offered to Sharp to put his collection on show. But Sharp did not want to part with anything for a second. He *did* make copies of some letters available to Whitehouse when he was working on *Vindication*, and I remember Sharp's anger and the rift which their unacknowledged publication brought. Later, Sharp was to deny Whitehouse and Evans permission to include the 1830 and the "Brantwood" diaries in their edition.

By this time, Sharp and Helen Viljoen had discovered each other. Sharp had material of vital importance to her study of the Ruskin family history, and he saw her as someone who would use his material in the way he would wish. An earlier will of Sharp's had left everything he owned to Mrs Holmes. Very soon after I returned to Bembridge in 1957, Sharp died and it was his dying wish, expressed to Mrs Holmes, that Helen Viljoen should have his Ruskin manuscripts. Mrs Holmes was going blind, and my mother went to Westgate Road to help her prepare the lists of books to be sent to Helen and to arrange for the disposal of non-Ruskin material (Sharp was a remarkably omnivorous collector!). Eventually, Helen Viljoen came to England in 1959 to collect the Sharp bequest. She took back with her to New York the manuscripts and some of the printed books and pictures. And Mrs Holmes decided that the collection at Brantwood should also be the final repository for other material. Much of this material she gave to Brantwood, but there were other items for which she thought Brantwood should pay, and a fair offer was made and accepted.

Arches at S. Maria Novella, Florence, by H. R. Newman, from the Ruskin and Sharp Collections

Thus it was that my parents eventually arranged for the removal from Barrow to Brantwood of two of Ruskin's mahogany bookcases that had formerly been in the old dining-room at Brantwood, a couple of fire screens, and a small single-pillar occasional table that had come out of the turret off Ruskin's bedroom. Drawings by Ruskin included his 1835 study of St Mark's and the Ducal Palace (Brant 1955), the delightful watercolour of the Palazzo Dario, Venice, 1846 (Brant 1035) and a number of the original drawings for plates in *Stones of Venice* which had previously belonged to Herbert Severn. Other items of Ruskin's included a blue satin wallet embroidered with his initials, the frame for his mother's eyeglasses (subsequently stolen), Ruskin's seal, and the Brantwood Visitors Book 1901–19 (Bem R 35). Here too was the 1840 cameo of him (Brant 721). The watercolours belonging to Ruskin included W. H. Hunt's still life of fruit, which formerly hung in the bedroom (Brant 735), a Hunt interior (Brant 734), Rooke's Auxerre, 1886 (Brant 769), Fairfax Murray's Calling of Matthew, after Carpaccio (Brant 752), and H. R. Newman's arches at S. Maria Novella, Florence (Brant 757). There was a large unfinished watercolour of the Mosque of the Sultan al-Ghuri, Cairo, by J. F. Lewis (which did not belong to Ruskin) and a number of Prout watercolours and drawings which did – Domo d'Ossola (Brant 761), two drawings of Ratisbon (Brant 765 and 766), the watercolour of Calais sands and pier, which was No. 1 in Ruskin's 1880 Prout and Hunt exhibition (Brant 760), and The English Cottage, in fact a cottage near Bridge End, Perth (Brant 762). This watercolour had a particular significance for Ruskin; it always gave the family pleasure and always hung "in the room most lived in". At Brantwood it lived in the study, above the door. In the preface to the Prout and Hunt catalogue, Ruskin wrote of the picture:

> The little drawing, bought I believe by my grandfather [who lived not far from Bridge End] hung in the corner of our little dining parlour at Herne Hill as early as I can remember and had a most fateful and continual power over my childhood mind. Men are made what they finally become only by the external accidents which are in harmony with their inner nature. I was not made a student of Gothic merely because this little drawing of Prout's was the first I knew; but the hereditary love of antiquity, and thirst for country life, which were as natural to me as a little jackdaw's taste for steeples or dabchick's for reeds, were directed and tempered in a very definite way by the qualities of this single and simple drawing.

The English Cottage by Prout, originally bought by Ruskin's grandfather

I subsequently catalogued the substantial number of books that had been at Brantwood and were then returned there from the Sharp collection in *Brantwood: Books from John Ruskin's Library*, 1967. Other material that returned to Brantwood now included a number of pieces of Cypriot pottery. In 1874–5 Ruskin helped to finance General L. P. di Cesnola's excavations to the tune of £1,000. In return, Ruskin received a number of antiquities of various sorts from the Cypriot dig. Some he gave to Oxford, some he gave to W. G. Collingwood, and some were displayed on shelves surrounding the della Robbia Madonna and Child above the Brantwood study mantlepiece. These were presumably dispersed in 1930–31, probably to one of the local dealers from whom Sharp bought a number of examples. In the early 1950s Sharp bought a motor car and learned to drive in order to be able to visit Brantwood regularly. He became friendly with Edgar Graham, who was the caretaker there then, and he gave him some of these Cypriot antiquities, which Graham in turn passed on to Brantwood (Bem R 43–58).

A number of years later, in 1971, four of Ruskin's 1834–35 copies after his watercolour master A. V. Copley Fielding, from the Sharp collection, were deposited on permanent loan at Brantwood by Mr E. Millard, in memory of F. J. Sharp and S. J. Millard. The Sharp material made a very significant addition to the collection at Brantwood. Remembering Sharp's stories of his purchases from the Grasmere dealer Thomas Telford, who bought before and at the Brantwood sale, I thought I would call and see if, after nearly 30

Part of Ruskin's collection of early Cypriot pottery

years, he still had any Ruskin material in stock. It was probably in the summer of 1958 or 1959 that I first called on Telford. He was talking to another customer when I arrived and, on looking round, I found a bookcase which was full of books by Ruskin or from Brantwood. I remember particularly Ruskin's own extensively annotated copy of *War*, one of the scarcest of his books. When I eventually introduced myself to Telford and explained that I was from Bembridge, I was almost forcibly ejected from the shop! As I left, Telford was still muttering about Whitehouse's refusal to buy the Ruskin family miniatures and silhouettes from him in 1931! I persevered, and visited the shop again before I returned to the south. This time I was allowed to stay – but the bookcase had gone and so had almost all the books. It was largely an academic loss, so to speak, because at that time the galleries had no purchase funds. However, I did find Ruskin's own set of *Fors Clavigera* and *Arrows of the Chase*, which I bought for my personal collection.

By the summer of 1960 I had limited funds for the gallery and I visited Telford again, buying an interesting collection of material. The 15 printed books from Ruskin's library which I bought for £3 10s. included Reichard's *Itinerary of Italy*, annotated and used by the Ruskins on their early tours, and a copy of *Sermons, principally … delivered in St Matthew's Chapel, Denmark Hill*, 1836, by Rev. Thomas Dale, who ran the academy in Grove Lane, Camberwell, where the young Ruskin had learned Latin and Greek.

On the same visit, a further £10 bought a number of Brantwood, Severn and Ruskin photographs, 17 small sketch-book leaves with sketches by Ruskin, 7 small sketches by Ruskin and 15 by Severn, a group of 11 copies of initials from medieval manuscripts, and 2 illuminated addresses to Ruskin from the girls of Cork High School, where Ruskin had established a Rose Queen's Festival, like his May Queen Festival at Whitelands.

I returned on at least five other occasions, and always found something of interest, despite Telford's protestations that he had nothing left. There were a few more of Ruskin's copies of his own books and pamphlets, including copies of the catalogue for the 1869 exhibition, *Flamboyant Architecture of the Valley of the Somme*, and the 1870 Verona catalogue. I found 15 mixed and mostly damaged examples of Brantwood cutlery and a seal which Telford assured me was Effie Ruskin's. It is certainly engraved E.R., but Mary Lutyens told me that she had never seen it used on any of Effie's letters. On one visit I bought Telford's own annotated copy of the 1931 Brantwood sale catalogue and the certificate of Ruskin's appointment as a member of the Académie Royale des Beaux-Arts d'Anvers (Bem L 23/A).

My last visit was in 1968. By then there really *was* nothing left from 1931, although even on that visit I made an interesting find. In a drawer I found Sara Anderson's Brantwood library catalogue. Telford insisted on *giving* this to me *personally*, saying that he thought it would be dangerous for such a catalogue to fall into the wrong hands. I thought this was amusing coming from Telford, in whose shop I had found so many books containing spurious Ruskin bookplates!

A bookseller in the north from whom I had been buying Lake District books for my own collection since the mid-1940s was Leslie Brookes of Kendal. A visit to him in the summer of 1964 produced a copy of *Remarkable Passages in Shakespeare*, 1870, by Ruskin's friend and near neighbour at Coniston, Susan Beever. On the same visit I bought a copy of Collingwood's *Limestone Alps of Savoy*, 1884, which was intended as a supplement to Ruskin's *Deucalion* and which I knew we did not have in the collection. But the real find of that visit was Ruskin's copy of J. O. Westwood's *Facsimiles of the Miniatures & Ornaments of Anglo-Saxon & Irish Manuscripts*, copy number 65 of an edition of 200 published by Quaritch in 1868. Not only is this an interesting and valuable book in its own right, but this copy is a prime example of how Ruskin used (or misused) his books. All the plates are loose and the top and bottom of the volume have been sawn off by Ruskin or one of his assistants to enable it to fit the appropriate shelf – fortunately, as it happens, or it would not have fitted my deepest shelf at Bembridge!

Haddon C. Adams was an engineer, the Ministry of Transport's chief bridge engineer. His book, *Reinforced Concrete Bridge Design*, 1933, is a classic in its field. He was introduced to the delights of Ruskin by Quiller-Couch when he was an undergraduate at Cambridge. He bought selectively but extensively from Brantwood in 1928 and again at the 1930–31 sales, though apart from keeping up-to-date with new publications, he does not appear to have added much to his collection subsequently. At the 1946 Ruskin Society luncheon Adams presented Christ Church, Oxford, with the certificate of Ruskin's appearance before the Vice-Chancellor, his subscription to articles and his oath of obedience to the university, his matriculation, his sponsoring certificate, and his public examination in Greats. Although Whitehouse did not realise the scope of Adams's collection, it was generally known that he intended to bequeath it to Bembridge. I visited Adams at his home in Merton Park in 1964 and was shown what I later discovered was but a small part of the collection. He had decided to give us some pieces that would otherwise have formed part of the bequest, and I came away with a watercolour study by Ruskin of the Ilaria di Caretto effigy at Lucca (Bem 1366), two documents relating to Catena's portrait of Doge Andrea Gritti (Bem MS 67), G. Salomon's *La Statue de Milo*, 1878, inscribed by the author to Ruskin, and Ruskin's travelling writing-case, which, according to Arthur Severn, was the only piece of luggage that Ruskin ever packed. While at Merton Park, I had seen and enthused about the Ruskin family Bible which Collingwood had described in *Ruskin Relics*, a Bible inscribed by Margaret Ruskin to her husband, and Rose La Touche's book *Clouds and Light*. Adams must have thought about these three volumes, which he then sent to the galleries in May; he followed this gift four years later with John James Ruskin's diary for 1833 and 1846 (Bem MS 33A).

I have been interested in the portraits of Ruskin for many years. My article on the portraits in the Whitehouse collection was published in *Apollo* in December 1960 and was followed six months later by a second piece on 14 other easily locatable portraits. The portraits have developed into an almost lifelong search and study.

In 1964 I was attempting to locate the original (as opposed to the plaster cast copies) of Benjamin Creswick's bust of Ruskin, modelled in 1877. Creswick came from Sheffield and had been introduced to Ruskin by Howard Swan. At Oxford Ruskin had met Queen Victoria's youngest son Prince Leopold, and when the prince visited the Guild of St George Museum at Walkley, Sheffield, in 1879, the Creswick bust was presented to him. It occurred to me that the bust might still be in the royal collection. Accordingly, I wrote to the prince's daughter, Princess Alice. The reply was that she did not have the bust, but she did have a small watercolour of ferns growing around a rock at Brantwood which Ruskin had given to her mother when encouraging her appreciation of watercolours. If I cared to have it for the collection, and to come to Kensington Palace to collect it, I was welcome. The attractive little drawing was duly collected and added to the collection (Bem ADD F/7). It was not until later that I realised that the original Creswick bust, modelled in plaster, was already at Bembridge (I had always taken it for one of the cast copies). Following a Victorian practice, it had probably been returned to Ruskin on the death of Prince Leopold in 1884, and bought at the Brantwood sale by Brown.

William Gershom Collingwood, son of the artist William Collingwood, came under Ruskin's influence as an undergraduate at Oxford. He was an accomplished artist and author, an archaeologist and authority on Norse lore. On leaving Oxford, he dedicated his life to Ruskin's service, becoming one of his secretaries. He continued to act as an assistant to Ruskin and Joan Severn up to and after Ruskin's death.

As well as being interested in the Creswick bust, I was also in correspondence with Mrs Gnosspelius, Collingwood's sculptor daughter Barbara, and *her* daughter Janet, also initially about portraits. I knew of the two 1897 portraits of Ruskin by Colling-wood. There is one in the Coniston Museum and an almost identical one at Bembridge (Bem 163). However, Cook and Wedderburn's Catalogue of Portraits also listed an oil sketch of the head for the two finished versions. I had searched unsuccessfully for this sketch and finally, in desperation, I asked Janet Gnosspelius if *she* knew where it was. "In the drawing room at Lanehead", she replied, "where would you expect it to be?" It always pays to look in the obvious place first!

So, on my next visit to Coniston, Janet Gnosspelius took me to Lanehead to see the portrait. Lanehead was incredible. It was little changed from Collingwood's time. Not long afterwards, Mrs Altounyan (Collingwood's daughter Dorothy) died and the family gave up Lanehead. The contents were to be dispersed and Janet Gnosspelius agreed to take me there again to have a look around the house. In advance, I made a list of things that I knew Ruskin had given Collingwood and that I hoped to find – I found them all and much else besides. It was suggested that I should make a list of anything that interested me, itemised, with my offer – which I duly did. My list was eventually returned, having been discussed by the Collingwood family. Rather unfairly, I thought, I was allowed to buy anything *below* a certain value; above that value, the pieces were going to Sotheby's.

I was able to add a lot of books to the collection: *The Ruskin Birthday Book*, inscribed by Ruskin to Mrs Collingwood, *Hortus Inclusus*, inscribed by Susan Beever to Collingwood, a part of *Our Fathers have Told us*, annotated by Ruskin, and *Storm Cloud of the Nineteenth Century*, with useful annotations by Collingwood. There is a copy of *Præterita* with Collingwood's annotations, and a copy of the 1880 edition of *Seven Lamps* with the 1891 privately printed *Index*; also, usefully, was a set in parts of Wise's *Bibliography of Ruskin*. Ruskin made frequent gifts of books to Collingwood, and I found and acquired several volumes on geology which fell into this category. I also got four folding maps of Switzerland which had belonged to Ruskin or his father.

Giacomo Boni was an architect and director of works for the Ducal Palace in Venice; he later became famous for his archaeological work on the Forum in Rome. Ruskin commissioned some watercolours of Venetian architecture from him, and at some stage Collingwood met him. They shared common interests and I found seven pamphlets or off-prints from learned journals inscribed by Boni to Collingwood. Angelo Alessandri was another of Ruskin's Venetian copyists whom Collingwood would have known. Here were copies by him after Bellini's Truth with her Mirror (Bem 1), Stefano's Crowning of the Virgin (Bem 7), del Fiore's Paradise (Bem 4) and Carpaccio's Meeting of Solomon and the Queen of Sheba (inscribed by Ruskin: "This is my own chosen one"; Bem 3), all given by Ruskin to Collingwood.

Collingwood, of course, wrote much about Ruskin and edited a number of his books. Here were the partial proofs of his *Limestone Alps of Savoy*, 1884 (Bem MS 67), a set of corrected proofs for Collingwood's 1891 edition of Ruskin's *Poems* (Bem MS 70), bound by the editor in a piece of heavy curtain material, corrected proofs of *Verona and Other Lectures*, 1894 (Bem MS 71) and *Lectures on Landscape*, 1897 (Bem MS 72). Also on my list was a copy of the 1900 edition of Collingwood's *Life of Ruskin*, inscribed to his wife, and a copy of the catalogue of the 1904 Manchester Ruskin exhibition, which he arranged, with many invaluable annotations. I found a watercolour geological survey of the Brantwood estate which Collingwood had drawn in 1882 (Bem 161), which has subsequently proved very useful in tracing watercourses and paths; and in the cellar I found several casts of Barbara Collingwood's smaller bust of

Ruskin – most of them were damaged, but I found one that was perfect.

Finally, I came across a nineteenth-century Persian manuscript *Diwan* of Mushtak, which Ruskin had given to Collingwood and which *he* had given to his daughter Dora. The manuscript was disbound, with only the remains of the spine present – clearly it had been so ever since it left Brantwood. I remembered that, among miscellaneous material (which must have been included with other things that had come from Brantwood), we had a painted board from a Persian binding. Out of curiosity, I compared this with the *Diwan* and, by the sheerest coincidence, the shredded leather fragments on the spine and on the board fitted. The two had become separated at Brantwood, possibly in the 1880s, and were reunited at Bembridge in 1965. Bayntun of Bath eventually rebound the manuscript, incorporating the one original board in their work.

The part of the Collingwood collection that was put into Sotheby's came up in February 1966. I was unable to buy the oil sketch for Collingwood's portrait of Ruskin. That went to San Francisco, to the antiquarian bookseller Warren Howell (a very distant relation of Ruskin through one of the Richardsons). But I *was* able to buy four drawings by Ruskin: a watercolour study of the Ilaria effigy in Lucca (Bem 1368), a study of a shaft of the main door of the Duomo in Lucca (Bem 1362), geological sections of Switzerland and the Lake District (Bem 1298) and the 1835 pencil sketch of a street scene in St Gall (Bem 1477). I was particularly pleased to get this last drawing, because we already had (Bem 1476) the finished pen and ink drawing worked up from the sketch.

Almost all Sotheby's picture sales in those days began at 11 o'clock. Very occasionally, as in this case, they began at 10.30, but most habitués of the rooms did not trouble to read the details carefully, and they turned up for 11 a.m. As *Fors* would have it, the lots in which I was interested came up at about 10.55, and I had to pay less for them than I had originally offered.

My regular perambulation in London has always taken me through Cecil Court, with visits to several booksellers. A shop that I had *not* visited before was that of E. Seligman. However, in December 1968 I went in and asked for Ruskin material. It turned out that, a number of years before, he had bought the remains of Williams Ward's papers. Ward had been a member of Ruskin's drawing class at the Working Men's College and had gone on to become a drawing master at the college. He also helped Ruskin by teaching some of those who applied to Ruskin for drawing lessons. When Ruskin was sorting out the drawings of the Turner bequest, Ward, in conjunction with George Allen, helped him. Allen and Ward also travelled on the Continent with Ruskin and William Ward became the most competent of the various Turner copyists employed by Ruskin. His copy of the bridge at St Maurice (Bem 595) is a very nice example of his work which came from the Maas Gallery in 1976. I think Ward went on to become a bookseller; just as George Allen became Ruskin's publisher, Ward became the officially appointed agent for the various series of photographs which Ruskin issued.

The collection already contained a number of Ruskin's books and pamphlets which had belonged to Ward, with his manuscript catalogue slips still in them. From Seligman I was able to buy a set of five of Ruskin's "Lesson Photographs", inscribed by Ruskin with his instructions to Ward. There was also a list by Ward of a proposed series of photographs to illustrate *Stones of Venice* (Bem MS 85). I was particularly pleased to get a copy of the printed folio introductory sheet to the series of photographs issued to illustrate *The Shepherd's Tower*, part VI of Ruskin's *Mornings in Florence*. The whole work, a series of 29 photographs, was issued with the printed introductory sheet, in a half morocco folder, in 1881. This is one of the relatively few earlier items that is not in the collection.

Reference to the Accessions Register reminds me that I was in London again a couple of weeks later, on New Year's Day, 1969. The day before I bought the Ward material, "Peterborough's" column in the *Daily Telegraph* had contained a reproduction of Geoffrey Fletcher's pen and ink drawing of Ruskin's birthplace, 54 Hunter Street, Brunswick Square, in London, coupled with the news that the house was to be demolished. The original of Fletcher's drawing was already sold, but he made another for the collection

Celebrating the 150th anniversary of Ruskin's birth, 8 February 1969. Left to right, R. G. Lloyd, C.B.E., Q.C. (later The Lord Lloyd of Kilgerran), J. S. D., Don Manuel Domecq-Zurita, Luis Gordon Snr., Luis Gordon Jnr. Manuel Domecq is signing one of the celebratory bottles of sherry

(Bem 193). I visited the house on 1 January 1969 – as it happens, in the company of Spike Milligan, who was also seeking preservable relics. *He* had done this sort of thing before and knew what he was looking for. Nevertheless, I was able to secure a number of interesting pieces – the glass and brass door knob and shutter knobs from the drawing-room, the brass chain and slide off the front door, a bedroom fireplace, and the Royal Society of Arts commemorative plaque from the façade of the building. This was eventually set into the wall above the galleries' terrace door, above an explanatory tablet cut in Coniston stone by a member of the Bembridge School staff, John Gower (who, it turned out, was also a talented letter-cutter). I was able to arrange for Coopers to make a photographic survey of 54 Hunter Street before the demolishers moved in, and these photographs are now in the collection with plans and other documents relating to the house (Bem MS 84).

The 1960s had been a fruitful period for Ruskin studies and for the galleries. The new era of Ruskin scholarship had begun. More than 20 books had been published. Ruskin exhibitions had boomed. The Arts Council had sponsored the first of the modern ones in 1954. This was arranged by Old Bembridgian Graham Binns and 10 of the 41 exhibits came from Bembridge. The small 1960 and major 1964 Arts Council exhibitions were both inspired by Kenneth Clark, himself something of a Ruskin collector; Bembridge lent half the exhibits in 1960 and, to the 1964 show, arranged by Elizabeth Davison, we lent 104 of the 394 exhibits. In the following year Helen Viljoen exhibited her part of the Sharp collection in New York, while in 1966 we lent 58 of the 93 exhibits in Terence Mullaly's "Ruskin a Verona", the first Ruskin exhibition held in Italy.

To celebrate the sesquicentenary of Ruskin's birth in 1969, I arranged an exhibition which was the first of several to be held in the offices of Luis Gordon, the importer of Domecq sherry and at that time the equivalent of Ruskin, Telford and Domecq. Other exhibitions in this landmark year were at Kendal and Sheffield (we lent 48 out of the 96 exhibits) and at the Central School of Art and Design, where Nikolaus Boulting (son of one of the successful Boulting brothers) arranged a Ruskin and Venice show, taking all 45 exhibits from Bembridge.

The year also saw a Ruskin conference at Brantwood. For a week, Ruskin scholars from England, America, Japan and Spain spent a hectic time at Brantwood lecturing and discussing Ruskin into the small hours. The week ended with the formation of the Ruskin Association, which was to act as publisher for the new *Ruskin Newsletter*, a periodical publication intended to keep international Ruskinians in touch with each other.

The 1960s had probably been the busiest decade for the galleries and the world of Ruskin since the 1930s.

The Ruskin Conference group at Brantwood, March 1969. Left to right, J. S. D., P. Messenger, Al Cate, Sam Brown, Laurence Johnson, Robert Hewison, Malcolm Hardman, Pierre Fontaney, P. Hammond, Hal Shapiro, Masami Kimura

CHAPTER XI

1970 TO THE PRESENT

Haddon Clifford Adams died on 14 June 1971. Writing in 1931 to Quiller-Couch, who had probably introduced him to Ruskin's writings at Cambridge, Adams said: "Collecting Ruskin is my one luxury." He and his wife had made Coniston the focal point of a motor-cycle holiday in the summer of 1928. During their several days in the village, they visited Brantwood on three occasions. They met Joe Wilkinson, the gardener, and his wife, who gave them tea in the Lodge, and they met Wilkinson's nephew Miles, the general factotum, who showed them around. They were able to see the gardens, and Violet Severn hoped that they had enjoyed their visit to the house.

Mrs Wilkinson gave Adams a copy of the *Magazine of Art* containing one of M. H. Spielmann's articles on Ruskin portraits; in an antique shop in the village he "picked up a few early sketches of Ruskin's" which were later authenticated by Miles Wilkinson. He arranged for Joe Wilkinson's daughter Edith to make two samplers for him, incorporating Ruskin lace.

Adams and Miles Wilkinson kept in touch, and after Adams had bought various lots, including John James Ruskin's watercolour of Conway Castle (Bem 458) at the 1931 picture sale at Sotheby's, he wrote to tell Wilkinson of his success. Wilkinson promptly sent him three more watercolours by J. J. R. as a gift (Bem 457, 459 and 460).

Adams must have told Wilkinson about his interest in books; Mrs Wilkinson promptly offered him some and, in packing the parcel, Miles put in a few more "and a few more small items", so that the parcel would travel better! Towards the end of June 1931 Adams visited Brantwood again and probably bought more books and perhaps some Ruskin letters. He marked his copy of the Brantwood sale catalogue with commissions which he left with Miles Wilkinson, but he was only successful in buying the walnut and rosewood occasional table which Ruskin used as a writing table in the dining-room. Thereafter Adams always used it as his own desk.

196 *But he gave the table to Brantwood about 1935.*

Conway Castle by J. J. Ruskin, formerly in Ruskin's bedroom, from the Adams Bequest

With the exception of new publications and a group of Ruskin–Leighton letters (Bem L 82), Adams does not appear to have had added to his collection after the sales.

During the war, much of the Adams collection was packed away for safety; when I visited him at Merton Park in 1964 I only saw a small part of it. Not until the bequest arrived at Bembridge in September 1971 and I began to unpack it, did I realise its full extent; I subsequently surveyed it in detail in the *Bulletin of the John Rylands University Library of Manchester* (vol 55 / no 2, Spring 1973).

The Adams bequest contained 410 items – letters, manuscripts, books, drawings. Adams had made a good selection from Brantwood, acquiring significant items. For example, there were letters to Ruskin from 58 different correspondents, including Henry Acland, Rawdon Brown, the Brownings, the Burne-Joneses (on the death of J. J. R.), Carlyle, Kate Greenaway, Jean Ingelow (with a holograph manuscript of her sonnet *Though all Great Deeds*), Edward Lear (and his manuscript dedication and corrected proofs for *Landscape Illustrations* for Tennyson), C. E. Norton, George Richmond, Joan Severn, Swinburne (with the manuscript of his poem *Itylus*), and his mother. Most of these were letters which Ruskin considered particularly important; many are enclosed in envelopes which he has endorsed with the correspondent's name and sometimes the subject

– and some are marked with a "D", probably indicating that Ruskin intended to print them in *Dilecta*. There were letters from Jane Carlyle and Samuel Prout to Ruskin's father and from J. A. Froude to Joan Severn. Letters from Ruskin are addressed to Dawson Herdson, his head gardener, Fanny Talbot, an early benefactor of the guild and of the National Trust, and Arthur Severn, including a letter telling him how he should conduct himself during his engagement to Joan Agnew.

There are two holograph manuscripts by Ruskin, the preface to *Hortus Inclusus* (Bem MS 91), and a note on a late conversation with his mother in 1871 (Bem MS 90); there was also a partly dismembered sketch-book of Ruskin's and a commonplace book which he used with his father in about 1830 (Bem MS 88). Manuscripts by others include Alexander Wedderburn's index to the translation of Plato's *Laws* and George Allen's statement for the cost and production of *Fors Clavigera*, 1871 (7,098 parts were sold, but sales steadily declined from 821 in January to 446 in December). From Ruskin's library there is a bound manuscript with drawings, *The Proportions of Ancient and Modern Architecture*, by the Regency architect of the National Gallery, William Wilkins.

There were three boxes of miscellaneous books by or about Ruskin, 185 volumes from Ruskin's library and an additional 50 with either Ruskin or Severn associations – Joan Severn's copy of Ruskin's edition of *German Popular Stories*, Arthur Severn's Latin dictionary (although he was more occupied in drawing boats on the end papers), and Susan Beever's copy of *Harbours of England*. Among those belonging to Ruskin may be noted his father's prayer-book, used by Ruskin on the last occasion that he attended Coniston Church; the Chiswick Press edition of Sir Philip Sidney's *Psalter*, 1823, used by Ruskin when preparing *Bibliotheca Pastorum* II; his copy of Cruden's *Concordance*, 1865; Ongania's monumental work on St Mark's, Venice; Prout's *Hints on Light and Shadow*, 1848; and *Sketches at Home and Abroad*, 1844. Ruskin's copy of Rose La Touche's *Clouds and Light*, 1870, is unfortunately quite unannotated. Here is Morris's *Earthly Paradise*, inscribed by the author to Ruskin; Wordsworth's *Yarrow Revisited*, 1835, inscribed to Anna Braithwaite by Dora Wordsworth; and Coventry Patmore's *The Unknown Eros*, 1877, bound in blue velvet and with an extra title page illuminated for Ruskin by Patmore's daughter Bertha.

HORTUS · INCLUSUS

Preface.

The ladies to whom these letters were written have been throughout their brightly tranquil lives at once sources and loadstones of all good to the village in which they had their home, and to all loving people who cared for the village and its vale, and secluded lake, and whatever remained in them or around of the former peace, beauty, and pride of English Shepherd Land

Sources they have been, of good, like one of its mountain springs, ever to be found at need. They did not travel; they did not go up to London in its season; they did not receive idle visitors to jar or waste their leisure in the waning year. The poor and the sick could find them always; or rather, they watched for and prevented all poverty and pain that care or tenderness could relieve or heal. Loadstones they were, as steadily bringing the light of gentle and wise souls about them as the crest of their guardian mountain gives pause to the morning clouds. : in themselves, they were types of perfect womanhood in its content happiness, Queens alike of their own hearts and of a Paradise in which they knew the names and sympathized with the spirits of every Living Creature that God had made to play therein, or to blossom in its sunshine or shade. .

They had lost their dearly loved younger sister, Margaret, before I knew them. Mary and Susie, alike in benevolence, serenity, and practical judgment, were yet widely different, — nay, almost contrary · in tone and impulse of intellect. Both of them capable of understanding whatever women should know, the elder was yet chiefly interested in the course of immediate English business, policy, and progressive science, while Susie lived an aerial and enchanted life, possessing all the highest joys of imagination, while she yielded to

Ruskin's manuscript of part of his Preface to *Hortus Inclusus*

There are 49 drawings by Ruskin in the Adams bequest, and a number of others that *could* be his work. Generally they are a disappointing collection, but there are some particularly interesting ones – an early drawing signed and dated 1 September 1831, and an 1832 view of Tunbridge Castle. Eleven drawings date from the 1835 continental tour and they make a welcome addition to the collection, which already contains a lot of work of this date. There is one of the Venetian worksheets, of the Ca' d'Oro (Bem Add V/52), and a preparatory study of Gneiss rocks at Glenfinlas, 1853 (Bem Add G/26), for the finished drawing in the Ashmolean. The 1875 drawing of Malham, Source of Aire (Bem Add M/35), joins the four other Malham drawings already at Bembridge.

All the 102 drawings by other artists must originally have come from Brantwood. Two examples are Prout's drawing of Wakefield Church (Bem 397) and an ink and wash study of two figures by Reynolds (Bem 419) – at least, that is what Ruskin thought it was, and Joan Severn has inscribed it on the reverse "Original sketch by Sir Joshua" – but Sotheby's say it is Zeus with a Fainting Woman by Romney. There were 21 watercolours by Arthur Severn, including his copy of Turner's Flint Castle (Bem 547), Coniston Old Man and the Copper Mines Valley from Brantwood (Bem 506) – a fine large watercolour, this, with the cypress trees in the foreground, planted by Ruskin, although Severn has only painted five of the six that there were! Of the Herne Hill house, there is a nice large watercolour of the back garden (Bem 515) and two small ink sketches of the house on one sheet (Bem 514). Of the greatest personal interest to me was Severn's watercolour of Ruskin, Joan, Sara Anderson and Wedderburn sitting in the evening in the Brantwood drawing-room. I knew of this portrait from a reference in a letter from Arthur Severn to Spielmann in my personal collection. Severn describes Ruskin as reading to the group "by the light of six tall candlesticks" – but again he couldn't count beyond five! When I was editing Severn's memoir of Ruskin as *The Professor*, I looked for this portrait, wanting to use it as the frontispiece, but my search was fruitless. However, I turned over the loose drawings in Adams's portfolio – there it was (Bem 527).

Other artists whose work is represented here are Kate Greenaway, Isabella Jay, Laurence Hilliard, Thomas Wade, George Butterworth, J. W. Bunney, H. R. Newman, Angelo Alessandri, Frank Randal and

William Ward. The Adams collection was a magnificent bequest. New cases had to be built to accommodate the books. Fortunately, only six months earlier we had been given two of the large and six of the small mahogany cabinets of picture-frames made to house the Ruskin Drawing School collection. These frames were still empty and ready to provide a home for many of the Adams drawings.

Peter Evans was a solicitor and a member of the firm which had been Ruskin's solicitors. Over the years he had accumulated a large quantity of material relating to Ruskin and his books. In 1971 he was moving to a smaller house and no longer had room to store the material; so he passed it on to the collection at Bembridge. Invaluable additions to one part of the collection were 67 voucher copies of Ruskin's late editions, sent to the solicitors on publication by Allen. Also related to books and their production were coloured drawings for the title page and frontispiece of *King of the Golden River*, used in the later George Allen editions.

There was a line block of the Uhlrich profile of Ruskin and four engraved plates. Ruskin's drawing of The Coast of Genoa, already in the collection, was originally engraved by J. C. Armytage to illustrate Ruskin's poem "The Battle of Montenotte" in *Friendship's Offering* for 1844. The Armytage plate had been lost, so it was re-engraved for volume 2 of the *Library Edition* by M. E. Saddler. His plate was one of the four. Another was Armytage's plate of the

Arthur Severn's portrait of Ruskin reading Scott in the Brantwood drawing-room

tracery of the campanile of Giotto, engraved for the second edition of *Seven Lamps of Architecture*, and used again as the frontispiece to volume 8 of the *Library Edition*. Ruskin himself had engraved the original version of this plate. In fact, he engraved two versions of the plate. The one used in the first edition was replaced by Armytage's plate in the second edition. The rejected version by Ruskin was used opposite page 138 of volume 8 of the *Works* – and this plate is present. The fourth of this group of plates was also engraved for the second edition of *Seven Lamps* to replace Ruskin's original, this time by R. P. Cuff. The subject is part of the cathedral of St Lô.

Other work on the *Library Edition* was represented by two letters to George Allen from Herbert Bell, the Ambleside photographer who photographed much of the material at Brantwood for the edition. Here also was a large parcel of photographs of drawings and manuscripts taken for the *Library Edition*. There was also a number of proofs of *Library Edition* illustrations and a number of large, earlier engravings of Ruskin's drawings. Included in the gift was a collection of 197 glass negatives of drawings by Ruskin and others. These are particularly valuable to the collection, because in some cases the original drawings have now disappeared.

Also among the photographic material were 26 glass negatives, each measuring 15¾" x 11¾". In 1884 Arthur Burgess, the wood engraver, either photographed, or arranged and superintended the photographing on Ruskin's behalf, of all the carving which surrounds the north door on the west front of Rouen Cathedral. These superb negatives provide a marvellous survey of the doorway. The only set of prints I know was the incomplete set at Sheffield.

To complete the gift was a group of large diagrams by Ruskin and his assistants, drawn as visual aids for lectures. These joined those already in the collection to raise our holding of these diagrams to over 40.

The next few years saw but a few notable additions to the collection, other than keeping up to date with publications. However, there were a few nice purchases – a small watercolour by Lady Waterford, The Witch's Briar (Bem 604), and Albert Goodwin's watercolour of the cloister and graveyard of St Helen, Abingdon (Bem 198), bought in Coniston and perhaps dating from 1871 when Goodwin was staying with Ruskin at Abingdon. Maria Edgeworth's *Frank*, 1837, and *Early Lessons*, 1835, given by Margaret Ruskin to a

Carving around the doorway at Rouen. One of the plates taken for Ruskin in 1884

Richardson relation, were passed on to us by Warren Howell, who had eventually inherited them. A Bible given by Rose La Touche to a Mr and Mrs McLaren on their marriage was also given to us at about this time. Other purchases included three letters from Ruskin, manuscript instructions to the architect W. Marshall for a Guild Museum extension (Bem L 31), and Ruskin's evening dress suit, bought from a collector of Victoriana in Shepherd's Bush (lot 456 in the 1931 Warwick Square sale and still with the lot number attached). We bought two interesting watercolours by C. H. Moore, landscape painter and Professor of Art at Harvard – S. Giorgio

Maggiore, Venice, 1876 (Bem 371), much admired by Ruskin, and a view of Simplon (Bem 370), where Moore and Ruskin spent a few days in 1877. In the same purchase came a fine small Ruskin Venetian watercolour of the Zattere with the church of the Gesuati (Bem Add V/61), drawn in 1876 and given to Moore at this time.

1976 was a good year. In February and April the collection acquired items from Mrs D. Inman of Coniston. Mrs Inman was the daughter of Edward Woolgar, who had been born in the Isle of Wight but had lived in the north for most of his life, where he was a railwayman with the Furness Railway. He was stationmaster at Coniston from 1888 until 1902 and, following his retirement in 1920, he settled in Coniston. For some years he was the curator of the Coniston Museum. He knew Ruskin and the Severns, and was very proud of his association with the Brantwood circle.

Included in the gift were several books that had belonged to Ruskin or the Severns, together with letters from the Severns, Collingwood, Sara Anderson and others written to Woolgar (Bem L 89). Woolgar last saw Ruskin at Brantwood on 30 April 1899 and he wrote a brief account of his visit. He also wrote his account of Ruskin's return to Coniston Station from Seascale in Cumberland

Simplon, 1877, by C. H. Moore

Edward Woolgar's pencil note of Ruskin's return by train to Coniston in 1889

in June 1889 – his last rail journey – an account containing Ruskin's much-quoted "There's no place like Coniston". I printed these two short accounts for The Ruskin Association in 1977 under the title *No Place like Coniston*.

It was in August 1976 that I was able to buy the Rose La Touche portraits. The saga had begun in 1968, when I had a letter from Mrs Feodora Ward-La Touche, an elderly lady living at St Jean-de-Luz in France. She told me that she was a niece of Rose's and had two portraits of her by Ruskin, of which I was eventually able to obtain photographs. However, the correspondence stopped after six months and I assumed that Mrs Ward-La Touche had changed her mind about selling the portraits. There matters rested until May 1976, when I had a letter from Mrs Sheila Taylor of Poole, informing me of her great-aunt's death and inquiring if I was still interested in the Rose portraits. I was. I went to visit Mrs Taylor and discovered, to my delight, that there were not *two* portraits of Rose by Ruskin, but *three*.

Two of the images are quite similar and fairly well known. Her head is seen in profile, looking down and to the left. In one, possibly drawn in March 1862 in pencil and black and white washes, she is wearing a garland of flowers round her head; the other, drawn in ?1874, is a pure pencil drawing. This latter was copied by Juliet Morse and E. R. Hughes, and their copy has been reproduced a number of times. The third, and most attractive of the three portraits, had never been reproduced. It is a watercolour head, facing three-quarters right and probably dating from the late '60s or early '70s.

I made an offer for the three portraits which was accepted. I subsequently learned that Mrs Taylor had already had the drawings valued, and my offer exactly matched the valuation. Grants from the Purchase Grant Fund, the National Art-Collections Fund and Luis Gordon Ltd. made the purchase possible and the portraits came to Bembridge.

While Whitehouse and Sharp and Adams had been building their Ruskin collections in *this* country, Ryuzo Mikimoto, almost certainly unknown to them, had been busily doing the same thing in Japan. He was the son of Kokichi Mikimoto, who had invented the cultured pearl and who had risen from poverty to run a very successful industry. His son Ryuzo went to Kyoto Royal University, and there he was introduced to Ruskin's writings. He devoted his whole life to Ruskin, neglecting the family business. He visited Brantwood at least once, bought from Severn, and was photographed with him in Ruskin's bedroom. He built up an important collection of books, letters, manuscripts and drawings. In Tokyo's Ginza he opened a shop named Rusukin Bunko (The Ruskin Library). Here his collection was available to those who wished to see it, and on the second floor "Ruskin tea and home-made cookies" were served. Handicrafts were also displayed.

Mikimoto commissioned young sculptors to create new images of Ruskin. A statue was sculpted from the Glenfinlas portrait. A bust was copied from the Gutzon Borglum statue, and a series of beaten copper reliefs were produced from one of Ruskin's portraits of Rose La Touche.

In addition to this, Mikimoto and a small group of friends established The Ruskin Society of Tokyo, which published a regular monthly journal between 1931 and July 1937. They also published original works about Ruskin in English and Japanese, and translated much that had been written by and about Ruskin into Japanese.

Ryuzo Mikimoto neglected Kokichi's business concerns and consequently his children had to take an active role in the industry from an early age. As a result they did not share their father's passion for Ruskin until after Ryuzo's death on 6 February 1971, when his son, Mr Y. Mikimoto, and daughter, Mrs Yukiko Homma, discovered Ruskin for themselves, whilst clearing up their father's estate. In 1979, to commemorate the 160th anniversary of Ruskin's birth, they exhibited the collection in the hall of the Mikimoto store in the Ginza, later establishing a Ruskin Library and a trust in Tokyo to house and care for the collection.

Both Mr Mikimoto and Mrs Homma had joined the Ruskin Association on the introduction of my friend Professor Kimura, who was at Brantwood in 1969. During visits to England both Mr and Mrs Mikimoto and Mrs Homma had been to Bembridge. In sorting out their father's books and papers, they made a collection of duplicated printed books which they gave to the galleries. Now known as The Mikimoto Gift, the collection comprises 43 books in Japanese by or about Ruskin. The largest holding of such works in the West, it was catalogued for us by Masami Kimura.

Most of the accessions in the next few years merely kept the library up to date, or added cheap editions of works by Ruskin that we otherwise lacked, but we did find the occasional association item – a Parian ware model of the Ruskin Cross and the *Ruskin School Home Magazine* for 1906 and 1907, for example.

Some interesting non-Ruskin material came to Brantwood in 1979–81 from Mrs F. Riggs of Hawaii, a descendant of the Republican wood-engraver W. J. Linton, who owned Brantwood before Ruskin. She gave us two children's books written and illustrated by Linton, and the engraved wood-block of *Jack and the Beanstalk*.

Six more books by Linton followed, including four which he had printed himself after his emigration to America, at his Appledore Press, and finally two watercolours by Linton arrived – a fruit bowl, and Appledore Farm – and a set of his wood engraving tools.

Other watercolours and drawings bought at this time from the large collection that was doing the rounds of the London dealers were four examples of the work of Ruskin's friend Henry Acland, Chamouni: Mer de Glace, 1846 (Bem Misc A/9), Mont Blanc from Val d'Aosta (Misc A/10), Crossing the Glacier, c. 1860 (Misc A/13), and a Scottish study of about 1844, Rhum, Muck, Eigg and Skye (Misc A/14).

Following the death of her husband Peter Evans (from whom we had received much material in 1971), Mrs Evans gave us a useful collection of documents (Bem MS 102). Presumably they were the remaining legal papers relating to Ruskin – probate of Joan Severn's will, documents relating to Arthur Severn's will, the assignment of the lease of 23 Herne Hill from Ruskin to the Severns, and documents relating to the Banstead Common.

In the second chapter of *Præterita* Ruskin had written:

Also, I may note in passing, that for all their talk about Magna Carta, very few Englishmen are aware that one of the main provisions of it is that Law should not be sold; and it seems to me that the law of England might preserve Banstead and other downs free to the poor of England, without charging me, as it has just done, a hundred pounds for its temporary performance of that otherwise unremunerative duty.

Here was Ruskin's guarantee for £100 and the Banstead Common Preservation Committee's receipt for £20 in 1877 and £80 in 1885 – and other documents in the case of this little-known Ruskin byway. And in 1987 Ruskin's christening robe came to Brantwood from Mrs Evans.

For several years I had maintained a sporadic correspondence with Mrs Wiggan. She was a descendant of Ruskin's manservant of the 1840s, John Hobbs, who had emigrated to Australia and made a name for himself in local administration. I had edited a group of letters written to Hobbs by his brother-in-law, George Allen. In 1985 Mrs Wiggan sent us a charming sampler embroidered by Ruskin's mother when she was a small girl. In both alphabets she had embroidered the "U" and the "V" in the wrong sequence!

Margaret Ruskin's embroidered sampler

The earliest portrait of Ruskin, the study of him with his King Charles spaniel painted in 1822 by James Northcote, which used to hang on the end dining-room wall at Brantwood, was sold at Sotheby's on 20 May 1931. Thereafter it disappeared for a number of years, reappearing in 1951 in New York, when it was sold as a "dog" picture. Again it disappeared, this time for 36 years, finally emerging in Sotheby's sale of 18 November 1987 (lot 57), for which the estimate was £20,000 to £30,000. We very much wished to see this portrait return to Brantwood, but could not possibly afford it. Fund-raising proved fruitless in the month at my disposal. I managed to secure offers totalling £15,000, but despite speaking to all the principal grant-giving bodies, I could not raise the necessary balance. However, at the eleventh hour the National Heritage Memorial Fund paid the hammer price of £23,000 to enable the National Portrait Gallery to buy the portrait and loan it to Brantwood, where it may now be seen.

This period was a busy one for Ruskin exhibitions. There were small exhibitions at Oundle (1977), Lancaster University (1979), Thornbury, Glos. (1983) and Bembridge (1987), where in almost every case the exhibits were drawn from our collection. The first major exhibition of the period was arranged by Robert Hewison for the J. B. Speed Art Museum in Louisville. Ruskin and Venice was the subject of the exhibition and Robert Hewison produced a show which graphically illustrated the connection, and a catalogue which is one of the standard works on the subject. Jeanne Clegg, who had been working on Ruskin for several years and had a number of books and articles to her credit, arranged an exhibition for the Arts Council in 1983 which opened in Sheffield and travelled to Liverpool, Kendal and Oxford. The catalogue and exhibition examined the character of Ruskin and his art and thought. In 1988 I put together 173 exhibits from the collection illustrating Ruskin's connections with the Alps. The exhibition opened in the Historisches Museum in Basle and travelled to Schaffhausen. From there it went on to Lucerne and Sion. At its first two sites the exhibition had only a German language catalogue, but subsequently a French edition was published. From Sion, it went to France and Aix-les-Bains, and eventually to the Museo Nazionale della Montagna in Turin. For this Italian venue a much more sumptuously illustrated edition of the catalogue was produced. When the exhibition finally returned to England, it was shown for a month at The Fine Art Society's galleries in Bond Street. For this location, the Italian catalogue was reprinted and was supplemented by a pamphlet containing, among others, the original English versions of the introductory essays. The exhibits finally returned to Bembridge and Brantwood in 1991.

After the Ruskin Lecture, 8 February 1982, at Tallow Chandlers' Hall, left to right, the lecturer, Professor Van A. Burd, Mrs Burd, J. S. D., Anthony Harris, Master of the Guild of St George

While this exhibition was on its travels, Ann Sumner arranged an exhibition illustrating Ruskin and the English watercolour from Turner to the Pre-Raphaelites at the Whitworth Art Gallery in Manchester. This brought together a very interesting collection from various sources (we lent a number of drawings), and the exhibition was supplemented by a further gallery of miscellaneous watercolours from the Whitworth collection.

In 1990, in connection with the Guild of St George, I met The Very Rev. Peter Moore, then Dean of St Albans. Mrs Moore was a member of the Oldham family and, in their house in Herefordshire, they had a substantial collection of Ruskin material that had belonged to Constance Oldham, Ruskin's god-daughter. The outcome of the meeting was that in October 1990 I went to Herefordshire to bring back a car-load of material, in all just under 100 items. There is an extensive collection of books by Ruskin, some inscribed by him to Constance, others given by him to her parents. The Oldhams were long-established friends; in fact, Mrs Oldham was the sister of Edmund Oldfield, the friend of Ruskin's youth with whom he had collaborated on the work on the new east window for St Giles's Church, Camberwell in 1844. Also among the books were several about Ruskin and a polyglot Bible which had belonged to him and bore his signature dated 1838 and his 1888 inscription to Constance.

Constance Oldham had been educated at Winnington Hall and here were two of her note-books with notes on Ruskin's lectures there, and transcripts of his letters to the girls. There were four watercolours by Ruskin – the Bridge at Laufenburg (Bem Add L/72), Sunshine at Grindelwald, 1846 (Bem Add G/71), Winter Evening at Lucerne, 1863 (Bem Add L/70) and an 1881 watercolour of the Brantwood garden with a view of the lake (Bem Add C/69). Retained by Mrs Moore was an unpublished and unlisted view of the outside of Rosslyn Chapel drawn in 1838.

The largest (and most expensive) influx of material for many years took place in 1991 and 1992. Although this material came as two entirely separate purchases, the first as lot 214 in Phillips's sale on 14 November 1991 and the second as lot 130 at Bonham's on 22 June 1992, they can really be regarded as an entity. All the material had originally passed through Telford's shop in Grasmere and is a classic example of how important groups of documents can become separated. As soon as I read the description of the Phillips's lot,

I realised that I had seen it 30 years earlier in a box at Grasmere. I was not allowed to touch it or examine it, only to look at what I could see through the top of the open box. The material had been sold to a Mrs Mack.

It was a miscellaneous collection, but one which contained some very important biographical material. Indeed, it contained material which was intimately connected with items we already had in the collection. Here were Margaret Ruskin's household accounts, Smith Elder's accounts with Ruskin, Ruskin's pocket diary for 1873, some of his original music, and much printed material (including the menu for Joan and Arthur Severn's wedding breakfast) and several books from Ruskin's library.

There were also 257 letters written by or to Ruskin, Joan Severn, and others – five letters to Ruskin from Lady Mount Temple, five to Mrs Simon, and three to Susan Beever, a number of letters to Ruskin from his mother, Mrs La Touche, the Simons and others – all letters which slotted into series which we already held. Then there were letters from Francesca Alexander and her mother to both Ruskin and Joan Severn and a large number of letters and telegrams of condolence to Joan Severn on Ruskin's death. There was a long run of 35 chatty letters from Tom Richmond, George's brother, to

The Brantwood dining-room today, with Northcote's portrait of Ruskin as a boy looking down on to the dining-table. The sideboard from the Raven Gift is near the window

Margaret Ruskin and, perhaps most importantly, a series of ten letters written by John Simon to his wife when he was staying at Brantwood to care for Ruskin during his illness of 1878. These letters give daily reports on his patient, and in them one finds valuable clues as to the cause of Ruskin's mental breakdown. Was it caused partly by financial worry?

The miscellaneous nature of the lot at Bonham's six months later made it quite obvious that this collection of material also originated from Telford's shop. There were photographs of Ruskin and of Herne Hill; there was Ruskin's passport and another bank pass-book to go with the eight which were in the Phillips's lot (I think the only ones missing from our series now are the four which passed from Telford to Sharp and are now in the Pierpont Morgan Library); here too was a large group of cancelled cheques and Ruskin's last cheque book of 1889.

Following Ruskin's recovery from his 1878 illness, a group of his friends bought for him Turner's watercolour of the Splugen. Here are many papers relating to the fund-raising, purchase and presentation (nearly 200 allied letters and other material in connection with the Splugen gift followed the same route as the four pass-books, to the Pierpont Morgan Library). Here is the cheque for Meissonier's Napoleon – and Ruskin's account for it – and documents in the "Calvert Case" (except those in the Morgan). There are Joan Severn's reminiscences of her stay at Rose Castle with the Bishop of Carlisle, her copy letter book with letters from Ruskin to Mrs La Touche, Lady Mount Temple and others. There were a number of miscellaneous drawings, and the original Ruskin drawing for plate VI of *Stones of Venice* I, illustrating types of towers. A drawing of a fruit and vegetable gondola has been cut from our 1845 diary.

Then there was a large number of letters – 5 from Francesca to Ruskin and 28 from her mother to Joan Severn (with a further 6 to her from Francesca); 12 to Ruskin from Mrs La Touche, and 6 from Margaret Ruskin to her son, and from Ruskin to Susan Beever and the Mount Temples; 6 to Ruskin from C. R. Gregory and another half dozen to Joan – and more Simon correspondence: one from Jane Simon to Ruskin, 48 from Ruskin to the Simons, and 7 more of the 1878 series from John Simon to his wife. Such was the connection between the Phillips's lot and our holdings, and the Bonham's lot with both, that we could not possibly have ignored them.

And Ruskin continues to flourish. 1992–93 saw the loan of about 100 exhibits from the collection to the Ruskin and Tuscany exhibition. This was arranged by Jeanne Clegg and Paul Tucker and was seen at the Accademia Italiana in London, at the Ruskin Gallery in Sheffield, and at the Fondazione Ragghianti in Lucca. Before this exhibition closed, we had lent a number of exhibits to the John Ruskin and the Victorian Eye exhibition which was mounted in Phoenix and Indianapolis. We also had more than 150 drawings by Ruskin and 19 by other artists on loan in Japan at the John Ruskin and Victorian Art exhibition which I had arranged for the Tokyo Shimbun. This exhibition received a lot of attention in Japan. It was shown in Tokyo, Kurume, Nara and Utsunomiya, attracting more than 50,000 visitors.

Meanwhile, the Raven collection was given to Brantwood. Kate Smith, Ruskin's housekeeper in London, moved with him to Brantwood. After her marriage to John Raven, they lived in Coniston, where they were often visited by Ruskin. Between them, Kate Raven's grandchildren inherited or acquired an interesting collection of material which Dame Kathleen Raven sent to Brantwood following the death of her two brothers Jack and Ronald. Here is a half blue calf set of the *Library Edition* said to have belonged to Wedderburn, a Ruskin fire shovel, several pieces of furniture with carved panels by the Coniston School of Carving, two Arthur Severn watercolours, a second print of the 1872 photograph of Ruskin and his friends in Italy (the only other print I know of belongs to the Bunney family), an Alpine landscape by Ruskin, a first edition of *The Nature of Gothic*, with Ruskin's bookplate, eleven letters from Ruskin to Kate Raven, his tie, his razor, his handkerchief, his father's prayer-book, tea cups and saucers, a circular dining-table and three chairs, possibly from the Brantwood drawing-room, and a mahogany sideboard formerly in the dining-room – and much else. This is another very generous gift which greatly enriches the collection and also secures the preservation of the artefacts themselves.

A further recent gift of considerable importance is the editor and publisher's own copy of *The Spiritual Times* for 1829–30, one of the rarest pieces of Ruskiniana, which contains his first published work.

And what of the future? Lancaster University plans to raise a substantial sum of money to build a new Ruskin Library. This has

Part of the Upper Gallery in 1994, just before the pictures were re-hung for the 175th anniversary exhibition

been designed by MacCormac Jamieson Pritchard and will be built in a prominent position on the campus.

In addition to building the library, the fund-raising will also provide an endowment to secure its future, as well as the future of the collection and of Brantwood.

Thus the Bembridge part of the collection will return to the north of England. While Brantwood continues to form the international memorial to Ruskin, Lancaster will become the centre for scholars who are working on some aspect of Ruskin's life and career.

The enthusiasm and commitment of John Howard Whitehouse made all this possible.

FURTHER WORKS BY J.S. DEARDEN

Brantwood. Books from John Ruskin's Library. Bembridge: Yellowsands Press, 1967

Catalogue of the Pictures by John Ruskin and other Artists at Brantwood, Coniston. Bembridge: Education Trust, 1960

The Cunliffe Collection of Ruskin Drawings. *Connoisseur*, August 1969

Edward Burne-Jones, Designer to John Ruskin. *Connoisseur*, February 1969

Facets of Ruskin. London: Charles Skilton, 1970

Further Portraits of John Ruskin. *Apollo*, June 1961

The Haddon C. Adams Collection at Bembridge. *Bulletin of the John Rylands Library*, 55, 2, Spring 1973

(ed.), *Iteriad or Three Weeks among the Lakes*, by John Ruskin. Newcastle upon Tyne: Frank Graham, 1969

John Ruskin (Lifelines 15). Aylesbury: Shire Publications, 1973. 2nd edition, Brantwood Trust, 1981

John Ruskin and the Alps. Lancaster University, 1991

John Ruskin and Bernard Quaritch. Some additional letters. *Bodleian Library Record*, XI, 4, May 1984

John Ruskin and Illuminated Addresses. *Bulletin of the John Rylands Library*, 66, 2, Spring 1984

John Ruskin and Victorian Art (exhibition catalogue). Tokyo: Tokyo Shimbun, 1993

John Ruskin: Lakeland Tourist. *Cumbria*, August 1960

John Ruskin on Ice. *Country Life*, 2 February 1978

John Ruskin, the collector, with a catalogue of the illuminated and other manuscripts formerly in his collection. *The Library*, June 1966

John Ruskin e le alpi (exhibition catalogue). Turin: Museo Nationale della Montagna, 1990

John Ruskin et les Alpes (exhibition catalogue). Sion: Editions des Musées cantonaux, 1989

John Ruskin und die Schweiz (exhibition catalogue) Basel: Historisches Museum, 1988

John Ruskin's Art Collection, a centenary. *Connoisseur*, September 1971

John Ruskin's Bookplates. *The Book Collector*, 13, 3, Autumn 1964

John Ruskin's Camberwell. St Albans: Brentham Press for the Guild of St George, 1990

John Ruskin's *Salsette and Elephanta*. *The Book Collector*, Summer 1985

John Ruskin's Tour to the Lake District in 1837. *Connoisseur*, March 1968

John James Ruskin: Artist and Patron. *Journal of Pre-Raphaelite and Aesthetic Studies*, Fall 1987

The King of the Golden River, a bio-bibliographical study. In Rhodes & Janik (eds.), *Studies in Ruskin. Essays in Honor of Van Akin Burd*. Athens, Ohio: Ohio University Press, 1982

An introduction to the microfiche edition of *The Library Edition of the Works of John Ruskin*, edited by E.T. Cook & Alexander Wedderburn. Oxford: Oxford Microform Publications, 1986

Portrait of a Bibliophile – John Ruskin. *The Book Collector*, Summer 1972

Portraits of Rose La Touche. *Burlington Magazine*, CXX, 899, February 1978

A present from Coniston. *Country Life*, 30 September 1982

Printing at Brantwood. *The Book Collector*, Spring and Summer 1979

The Production and Distribution of John Ruskin's *Poems* 1850. *The Book Collector*, Summer 1968

(ed.) *The Professor: Arthur Severn's Memoir of John Ruskin*. London: George Allen & Unwin Ltd., 1967

Ruskin and Coniston, with drawings by Keith Thorne. London: Covent Garden Press, 1971

Ruskin Association Books. Bembridge: Yellowsands Press, 1962

The Ruskin Circle in Italy in 1872. *Connoisseur*, April 1972

The Ruskin Galleries at Bembridge School, Isle of Wight. *Bulletin of the John Rylands Library*, 51, 2, Spring 1969

Ruskin Galleries, Bembridge School, Isle of Wight. *Apollo*, December 1961

(ed.) *The Ruskin Newsletter*. Bembridge: The Ruskin Association, 1969–date

Ruskin on tour in Northern England and Scotland in 1838. *Apollo*, August 1963

Ruskin's Politics by Bernard Shaw. *The Book Collector*, Autumn 1971

An introduction to the microfiche edition of *Sale and Exhibition Catalogues relating to John Ruskin, his Work and his Collection*. Oxford: Oxford Microform Publications, 1981

A Short History of Brantwood. Coniston: Association for Liberal Education, 1967, 2nd edn., 1974

Some Portraits of John Ruskin. *Apollo*, December 1960

(ed. with Van Akin Burd), *A Tour to the Lakes in Cumberland. John Ruskin's Diary for 1830*. Aldershot: Scolar Press, 1990

Wise and Ruskin. *The Book Collector*, Spring, Summer and Autumn, 1969

INDEX